Confessions of a Prep School Mommy Handler

Confessions of a Prep School Mommy Handler

A Memoir

WADE ROUSE

Harmony Books • New York

Published in the United States by Harmony Books, an imprint of the
Crown Publishing Group, a division of Random House, Inc., New York.

www.crownpublishing.com

HARMONY BOOKS is a registered trademark and the Harmony Books
colophon is a trademark of Random House, Inc.

Library of Congress Cataloging-in-Publication Data
Rouse, Wade.
Confessions of a prep school mommy handler : a memoir /
Wade Rouse. — 1st ed.
p. cm.
1. Rouse, Wade. 2. "Tate Academy" (New York, N.Y.)—
Employees—Biography. I. Title.
LD7501.N528R68 2007
373.22'2092—dc22
[B]
2007004939

ISBN 978-0-307-38270-2

Printed in the United States of America

Design by Lauren Dong

10 9 8 7 6 5 4 3 2 1

First Edition

For Gary, my muse —
I promise "the dream" will get easier

"I am getting to know the rich."

"I think you'll find the only difference between the rich and other people is that the rich have more money."

—MARY COLUM'S RESPONSE TO ERNEST HEMINGWAY

Contents

Author's Note

To be perfectly transparent from the start, a personal disclosure: I highlight my hair. I do. I admit it. My real color is actually called "dirty dishwater." You'd highlight, too, with that literally hanging over your head. I love lattes. And, yes, I admit to fake-baking in the dead of winter. Otherwise, I look like I have scurvy.

I have also worked for many years in educational administration, in development and publicity capacities, including numerous years in higher education as well as two tenures in independent education. The experiences recounted in this book occurred during my employment in independent education. To protect privacy and anonymity, I have changed names and identifying characteristics of everyone portrayed in this book, with the exception of my family and me. I also rearranged and compressed events and time periods to better clarify the narrative. In some instances, I combined the characteristics and incidents of several different people into a single character to help streamline the story and to further mask identities. Accordingly, no individual should be presumed to represent any one person. For example, "Kitsy" is a composite of several Mean Mommies I knew; "Doty" is a composite of several administrators with whom I worked.

I have also changed the name and disguised the identity and location of the school. It's an incredible place and continues to be so because of the dedication and commitment of countless wonderful teachers, administrators, and parents. I chose to write about a select few of the people I worked with whose personalities overshadowed the incredible work of the majority. This situation is what we often refer to in nonprofits as the "five percent rule," whereby a subset of any group often requires constant attention and the remaining ninety-five percent are extraordinary human beings.

Part One

The Fall Semester

"When Maria finally appeared, she wasn't hard to spot. In this mob she looked like something from another galaxy. She was wearing a skirt and big-shouldered jacket of a royal blue that was fashionable in France, a blue-and-white striped silk blouse, and electric-blue lizard pumps with white calf caps on the toes. The price of the blouse and the shoes alone would have paid for the clothes on the backs of any twenty women on the floor. She walked with a nose-up sprocket-hipped model-girl gait calculated to provoke maximum envy and resentment. People were staring."

—SHERMAN McCOY,
The Bonfire of the Vanities, BY TOM WOLFE

Everyone in the (Car) Pool!

Deep cleansing breath iiiiinnnn . . .
Exhaling all the toxins . . .
Rrrriiiiiiiinnnnggg! Rrrriiiiiiiiinnnnggg!
Deep cleansing breath iiiinnnn . . .
Exhaling all the toxins . . .
Rrrriiiiiiiinnnnggg! Rrrriiiiiiiiinnnnggg!
Deep cleansing breath iiiinnnn . . .

I am wearing a Kenneth Cole suit, standing in the middle of my old, wide-windowed office at work, chanting and performing yoga breathing exercises. I am trying desperately to hear my inner voice, to hear only birds chirping and the sounds of ocean waves, but I can hear only the ringing of my phone. Blaring for the fourth time in less than two minutes.

I separate my hands, which are locked in prayer, and peer through them at the caller ID on my phone. *Her again?*

My knees creak as I sprint out the door, in a semipanic.

I'm already running late for afternoon carpool, running late for my mommy.

It is the first day of school at Tate Academy, one of the nation's most historic and revered private schools, where I serve as "the mommy handler," and working the carpool lane is an essential, occasional, yet ongoing component of my job, kind of like working a streetcorner is to a hooker. In truth, there are real similarities: Each of us doggedly protects our assigned turf and, by end of the day, each of us knows we're gonna end up screwed. In completely different ways, of course.

While my official and politically correct title at Tate Academy is Director of Public Relations, I was told that I was specifically hired to be "the mommy handler." Those were the odd but "secret" words that were used in my original interview not so long ago by someone who, of course, has since left the school. I know they were used somewhat facetiously, but there is still a ring of truth. And it doesn't take a linguist to dissect that phrase.

I . . .
handle . . .
mommies.

In essence, I am the bug guard on the institutional vehicle; I get whacked and splattered, take the hits, so everyone else riding in the car—the administration, the faculty, the staff, the students—stays clean and unharmed from annoying, stinging insects.

Working at a prep school, you see, is akin to being a beekeeper. You get stung enough times—like I have, like all faculty and staff do—and you always make sure to keep your protective gear on and zipped up tight. Frankly, you get a little paranoid. Because just when you are lulled by the sleepy hum of the buzzing or the richness of the honey—BAM!—the bees attack. It's just the natural order of things here, the way of the colony: I am half worker bee, half eunuch-drone.

Today, this first day of school, I am on my way to get stung by the Queen Bee herself: Katherine Isabelle Ludington.

Mrs. Ludington is my new liaison to the parent group *and* alumni group, the two groups whose work I help oversee. She summoned me to meet with her for the first time just a few minutes earlier. The sound of her clipped, every-syllable-is-overenunciated voice this morning set off my yoga-induced chanting, my last-ditch effort to center my mind and body. It didn't work, and I'm less than a day into the new school year.

I quickly snake my way along the worn brick path that runs alongside our cobblestone carpool lanes, sweating in the heat. It is 110 degrees in the shade. In the summer, the humidity of our city hangs in the air like fog—the result of being so close to a big body of water—and its heavy, hot wetness wilts you on first contact, making it difficult even to catch your breath in this American rain forest.

The reflection off the never-ending line of SUVs in carpool is blinding, and I did not bring my sunglasses—make that, *would* not bring my sunglasses—with me. Working at Tate Academy, I really need stylish new shades, hip shades, ones that make me look like I should be photographed on the town with my best pals Carson Daly and Christina Aguilera. The ones I own right now are from Target's children's section since my head is so small; they are the only ones I can find that fit. My sunglasses say "Sassy Girl" on the side. This just doesn't cut it style- or genderwise at Tate, but it sums up the odd dichotomy that is my life here. In this river of money, I am the gay salmon swimming against the current. Except, I try every day not to make a splash, to fit in with the other, prettier fish—the ones going the right way in the current—even though instinct tells me to swim like hell in the other direction.

I approach the carpool lane and squint into the sunny, shimmery sea of idling, just-washed black Land Rovers, Escalades, Excursions and Navigators, searching for Mrs. Ludington. Tate's carpool lane looks exactly like a new SUV lot, except for the fact that right here, right now every tinted window is cracked just enough to reveal a pink-clad Stepford army of tiny, tan blondes all riding high and gesturing wildly into Laffy Taffy–colored cell phones. Though this may sound like an overexaggeration, there is an eery sameness to this scene. And yet I can still easily pick out my speed-dialing mommy.

Mrs. Ludington has the dog who is dressed just like her.

I have seen the duo pictured together numerous times in the society pages of the newspaper at Humane Society fund-raisers and Animal Protection benefits. They come as a set—this blond heiress and her snow white sidekick.

The famed LulaBelle, Mrs. Ludington's "showdog," is a fluffy, white cock-a-poo-something-or-other for which I heard she paid ten thousand dollars. LulaBelle, who actually looks like a frayed athletic sock, is riding shotgun and yapping at anything that happens to move. Which is everything in carpool. LulaBelle is wearing pink doggles and a pink gingham bow on her collar, and a little pink tank top that says "My Dogs Are Barkin'." Even her little nails are painted pink. If she had opposable thumbs, I am quite confident LulaBelle would be on a cell phone barking orders to her maid and sipping a no-fat Starbucks iced latte just like many of these mothers.

Pink is a primary color for many Tate Academy mothers and pets. Lilly Pulitzer pink, to be exact. Pink is not an accent color here. It is not simply a pop of pink, like a begonia in a window box. It is *the* color. Tate's M²s (my secret acronym for the select few Mean Mommies with whom I am occasionally forced to work) will mix in a bright green with the pink—anything that looks like it might belong in a spring bouquet—but that is the extent of the fashion color wheel for the Mean Mommies here.

Oh, lipstick is pink, too. Specifically, bubblegum pink. The M²s still try to look exactly like they did in their high school senior class photos, the ones I make into blowups for their reunion parties. I am

knee-deep in these blowups right now. Tate masochistically schedules its Reunion Week just after the start of school, just after the end
of a peaceful summer. For me, the start of school every year is like
luging without a moment of training.

Mrs. Ludington has summoned me from my office to discuss "a
matter of vital importance." That's all she said before hanging up on
me the first time she called. The second and third times she called,
she asked, "You're still not on your way? This is vital!" I turned to
yoga and ignored her fourth call.

I will soon learn a lot of things from Mrs. Ludington, first and
foremost being that every matter is of "vital importance" to her: the
temperature of her water (room temperature, so her body can absorb
it more quickly), the texture of the paper on which our alumni magazine is printed (not "buttery" feeling enough), the lack of chickpeas
on Tate's salad bar ("Wade, I mean, please, how could you overlook
something like that? It's a perfect food, like the blueberry!").

As I approach her Land Rover, I can see her daughter being es-
corted to the mammoth SUV by an assistant teacher who looks like
a *Price Is Right* girl. Many of our teaching assistants at Tate—the
teacher's helpers—look like Uma Thurman. Being able to look hot
in trendy outfits and shoes while finger painting and wiping up puke
is as important, it seems to me, as a teaching degree from a private
university.

The little girl disappears into the back, in the third-row seating,
behind the tinted windows.

I walk cheerfully up to the Land Rover, waving like a hitchhik-
ing Moonie, and peek in the tiny opening of the passenger window.
The little girl smiles at me from the back. LulaBelle tries to remove
my nose through the crack in the passenger side window. By quickly
comparing resemblances, I think Mrs. Ludington actually gave birth
to LulaBelle and adopted the little girl.

"You're tardy," is how she greets me, like I'm a third-grader who forgot to get a bathroom pass. Still, I smile at this friendly welcome, like Dolly Parton has just welcomed me to her mansion with a big ol' hug and a cup of moonshine.

Though I have seen Mrs. Ludington numerous times—in meetings, on campus, in the newspaper, on TV—this is the first time I have actually looked this closely at her.

She is pretty-ugly. Not pretty ugly, in the adverb-adjective sort of a way, but a combination of the two opposing looks. Her face is delicate, her features attractive, but her proportions are not perfect, some elements a bit harsh. From a distance, she looks great. Up close, she looks like a Cubist painting, where everything's just a bit off.

Her eyes, however, are unforgettable; they are the color of a Blue Raspberry Mr. Misty from Dairy Queen. Her eyes have the ability to freeze you, instantaneously, coldly, like you licked an ice cream cone too quickly.

Mrs. Ludington is ensconced in a shrunken pink Lilly Pulitzer polo and pink floral-and-heart capris. She looks like an animated begonia, a floral DreamWorks character who has plucked herself from one of our window boxes and taken to the streets to find her long lost mother, the petunia.

Her body is as fragile as a flower's stem. Her hair is white blond, almost like snow, and sprayed into a helmeted bob. She is bronzy tan, vacation tan, not fake tan.

Despite her size, she exudes confidence. Whereas I am a leaky faucet drip of confidence, she is a virtual sprinkler of attitude. I can feel it emanate from the car. She carries herself as though she is six-foot-four—a good foot taller than her actual height—her attitude arriving a split second before her perfume (Dolce & Gabbana Light Blue), which drifts from the car like gas.

Mrs. Ludington and her family are old city money, old city conservatism, old city power. Mrs. Ludington was everything in her career at Tate Academy: beauty queen and sports star. She went to an Ivy, married an Ivy, and made a lot of money. Her life, in short, has been perfect. Is perfect. Or a constant quest for perfection.

That rather simple yet unattainable standard, in fact, sums up perfectly the private school where I work. We must always seek perfection.

Tate Academy is one of the oldest independent schools in the nation. Annual tuition today at Tate approaches the cost of one of these SUVs, not counting "extras," like books, clothes, computers, athletic uniforms, field trips. So, if you can come up with the cash and are comfortable attending school nude and with no supplies, you can probably scrape by here. Admission to Tate Academy is a privileged honor in our city, the equivalent of being tapped for sainthood. Very few make it onto this holy, sacred ground. I consider myself lucky to be at such a prestigious school.

In fact, Tate Academy has graduated so many famous alumni, so many VIPs, so many celebrities, so many movers and shakers, so many big names that you would gasp and ask, "They *all* went there?"

And they did. Which is exactly why I wanted to work at Tate in the first place. To be a mover and a shaker for once in my life. To be liked by the most popular people for once in my life. Sad? Yes. Pathetic? Yes. True? Yes.

What's truly pathetic is what I endure in this quest for acceptance. Occasionally working carpool, for starters. At Tate—at any private day school, for that matter—the carpool lane is often the center of M^2 activity. It is like a live electric wire, really. The gossip that buzzes through this endless line of gigantic, jumbotronic SUVs has cost administrators and teachers sleep. I often work carpool to ground that electricity, to take a jolt and then report its shock level to higher-ups.

Carpool is where the gossip starts, the rumor mill churns, the lies fly. I can literally see it happening before I even approach the lane. One mommy hopping out of her SUV and then jumping up and onto the running board of the SUV behind her to whisper something to that M². Or cell phones chirping all at once, Mozart or Britney Spears ring tones playing through cracked windows. That's when I know there is trouble brewing.

I have already held lots of meetings standing outside an SUV—making deals, bartering, begging, schmoozing, pleading, finally, reluctantly agreeing to a situation that makes me wholly uncomfortable.

I really am a hooker.

At least, I try and convince myself, I'm a high-class whore.

I often work the street, no matter the weather—in rain, or snow, or 110-degree heat, like an indentured mailman—conducting a meeting through a crack in the passenger-side window, all the while trying to keep up with an M²'s SUV without getting thrown under a tire as she alternately punches her accelerator and then slams on her brakes.

This little maneuver is, in fact, what jolts me out my reverie this afternoon, makes me remember too late that I am still staring at Mrs. Ludington. I can see her mouth moving—*Hello? Wade? Hello?*—but my synapses are not connecting her words.

It is too hot. I can't do this another year. Please, God, not another year.

To grab my attention, Mrs. Ludington proceeds to gun her Land Rover one more time with a pink espadrille, the SUV jolting forward, dragging my body alongside. I look at her, my eyes wild, my nails gripped to the top of the windowframe.

"I thought that might do the trick. My God, for a moment I thought you were in a coma."

Her Mr. Misty eyes freeze me.

"Let's cut to the chase, shall we? Wade, *your* Reunion theme and decor are simply too boring, as you have them planned," she says to me through the opening in the passenger window. No "I'm excited about working with you this year"; just a simple, direct "We need to 'rethink' it."

Who the hell is "we"? I want to ask. *Do you have a mouse in your pocket, sir?* I hear my mother say in the back of my head.

Instead I say, "Everything's ready to go, Mrs. Ludington. We're only weeks out."

That was too direct. Slow down. I am panicking and talking too quickly. I don't want to seem panicky. I must be peppy yet tough, direct yet respectful, flattering without being fawning. I have perfected this manner of speaking in my time at Tate; it works on rich mothers. So I add:

"Oh, and I just love your polo, Mrs. Ludington. Lilly Pulitzer, right?"

For some reason, this doesn't work on her. She is simply staring at me.

"Call me Kitsy," she says.

I am still leaning into the passenger-side window of her Land Rover, holding onto the top of the window like a dangling, suicidal window washer, my feet barely brushing the ground, too afraid to step foot on her shiny, polished running board. I say nothing, so she punches the gas once more, and her car jolts forward in the carpool line, me stumbling tippy-toed to keep up. She slides on a pair of pinky red Chanel sunglasses, which are only slightly smaller than her Land Rover, and turns to stare at me again. The air conditioner is on high and blowing LulaBelle's ears around like she's a high-priced model posing in front of a wind machine.

I can't do it. I can't make myself say it. It's just too ridiculous to say out loud. So she says it for me.

"Call me Kitsy."

No! I want to scream. That sounds like a nickname I would have been called by the mean boys in my country school.

I pray that she will suddenly say, "Call me Ishmael," anything, any name, other than this. But I smile and nod, as though it's the most charming nickname I've ever heard, like Lady Bird or RuPaul. That's typical at Tate, however, typical of our city's wealthy women. Bizarre childhood nicknames, fit for a cockatiel or Shih-Tzu, that stick for life, grown women forever calling each other Bitsie, or Foobie, or La-La, or Kazoo, as though it's the most normal thing in the world.

"Call me Kitsy," she says. Again.

"Will do!" I say enthusiastically.

"Kitsy," she encourages, like she's trying to teach a parakeet to ask for a cracker. "It's short for Katherine Isabelle. My grandmother is Itsy, short for Isabelle, my mother is Bitsy, short for Elizabeth Isabelle, and my daughter is Mitsy, short for Madeleine Isabelle. Isn't that just adorable?"

"So, is there a spider?" I ask, trying to make a little joke, add a little levity, act like I'm comfortable with this whole nickname thing. "You know . . . Itsy . . . Bitsy . . . Spider?"

How come when you've made a verbal gaffe, you don't realize it until it actually comes out and sits in the air, like one of those cartoon balloons? Even LulaBelle seems to notice, barking, "You're a moron" at me.

"Noooo," she says slowly, icily, drawing the word out as though she's getting paid royalties per second. She doesn't laugh. The only sound is the air conditioner, followed by the lowering of the passenger side electric window, followed by LulaBelle's barking.

"Say it," she commands. "Say my name, just so we know that we're off to a good start in our working relationship. It's going to be a very busy year, and I want us to be fast friends. Oh, I didn't see your shirt until now! Kenneth Cole, right? I absolutely adore it!"

This makes me deliriously happy for some reason. So I smile at her like a lunatic and say her name.

"Kitsy."

A trickle of sweat burns my eye and another runs into the corner of my mouth. I inhale the cold air coming from the SUV like it's the last, precious few ounces of oxygen. I am melting. And then it hits me. *Oh, my God! She pulled my flatter-don't-fawn trick on me, and it worked.*

"Good," she says. "I feel so much better. Don't you, Mitsy? Don't you, LulaBelle?"

Mitsy claps and LulaBelle barks. I quickly know that everyone must respond to Kitsy on command.

Still, I've managed to say her name, to survive my first test with her. Not my second, however.

"Soooo . . . as I was saying originally, I just had a chance to review your Reunion plans. Wade, the decor is gold and blue. It looks like a fund-raiser for Notre Dame. We are *not* a Catholic school. Change the colors and the background. And falling leaves are too . . . fall. It's still summer, am I right?"

Our school colors *are* gold and blue. They were chosen 150 years ago; I didn't just make them up for the hell of it. And the theme for Reunion this year is "Fall in Love All Over Again with Tate." Get it? Leaves . . . fall . . . reunion? Play on words? And, by the by, this was approved *three months ago by a committee of fifty.*

It is so hot that I have sweated through my shirt and suit jacket. It looks like I'm wearing extra-thick Lycra. Still, I say nothing. I just smile.

Kitsy begins dumping the contents of her Louis Vuitton Speedy 30 carryall into the passenger seat. LulaBelle dances excitedly over lipsticks and perfume bottles and credit cards and a thank-you note from the car dealership.

"Here," she says, holding out her tote to me. In trying to lower the window a bit more for me to see her purse, Kitsy "accidentally" hits the passenger window control, causing the window to close and crush my head. *She probably opted not to have a sensor on her windows, just for an occasion like this.*

"Oopsy," she says, unlocking the doors first, before rolling the window back down.

LulaBelle barks her approval.

I rub my head and look at the little girl. She is dressed exactly like her mother, too.

"Are you OK?" Mitsy asks me, rubbing her head in sympathy.

I smile at this gesture of kindness.

"So . . . Wade, what I want you to do is take my Louis bag and make the background for the brand new invite match their logo. Isn't it just brilliant?"

Are you kidding me? I don't even get it, except that she's obsessed with Louis Vuitton and wants to show off her new purse.

"I just came up with it over lunch at the Club. It's the best, right, Wade? It is speck-tack-u-larr, so let's do it!"

Question. Command.

Kitsy, I will quickly discover, has a magical way of asking a question that is really a command. I will term it the question-command, a trick I will try to master, especially in everyday life. Instead of asking, "Does a house salad come with the entrée?" you say, "A house salad comes with the entrée, correct? I couldn't imagine it being any other way!" Never give the listener a chance to respond. Never give them an option. Never give them an out. My next Kitsy question-command is this:

"I think addressing all of the Reunion invitations by hand is the only way to go, don't you, Wade? Doing it any other way would be so déclassé.

"Show me the mock-up tomorrow. We're weeks behind as it is now. Oh, and add pink in the motif. Pink, pink, pink! TTFN!" (Tate's M²s love to say "TTFN!" It's an acronym meaning "Ta-Ta for

Now," for those of us who have moved beyond passing notes in junior high that say, "Do you like me? Circle one. Yes? No? Maybe?")

And, with that, Kitsy screeches off, performing a U-turn in the midst of carpool—no small feat in a Land Rover and line of SUVs—like a rich, suburban Shirley Muldowney. LulaBelle is trained for this. Her pink nails grip the passenger door, her ears flapping in the SUV's cross breeze, her doggles making her look like a furry version of Kristin Scott Thomas in *The English Patient.*

I stand in the middle of carpool, a man holding a handbag, SUVs now tooting at me to move. I think of all the new work that is to come: revamping an invitation that doesn't need revamping, working for weeks on end hand-addressing and stamping invitations, and reorchestrating an entire Reunion that doesn't need reorchestrating.

But that's jumping ahead. Right now, it's only day one of the new school year.

I ignore the honks, clutch my new handbag tightly to my chest like a lost old lady in the middle of Times Square, and start chanting.

Deep cleansing breath iiiinnnn . . .

Exhaling all the toxins . . .

The Fall Guy

It is finally Reunion Week on campus at Tate, and I consider Reunion Week here to be akin to Hell. Except Hell has less vicious, less tan attendees.

Our big Reunion Week kicks off Tate's never-ending, yearlong event season. Reunion Week itself is a nonstop smorgasboard of parties—alumni BBQs, "hen parties" for women only, golf scrambles and new parent parties, and mixers for young alums. Tate backers swarm campus, expecting—make that demanding—perfection from a guy and many others who are a lot less than that.

I have made it to Friday unscathed. This is an accomplishment. My morning thus far has included running around taking photos of "Chips" (Chips off the Old Block), current Tate students who are legacy children, grandchildren, nieces, or nephews of reunion attendees; and, most importantly, escorting old women to the bar or the bathroom.

Most recently, I have been attending to Contessa Van Cleve. Mrs. Van Cleve is celebrating the seventy-fifth anniversary of her graduation from Tate. She has returned from a coastal village on the Eastern seaboard to be honored on her diamond reunion at today's luncheon.

When I open her limo door, Mrs. Van Cleve emerges looking

very much like an old, freeze-dried Morgan Fairchild. Indeed, ninety-three looks very much like fifty-three at Tate.

I extend my hand, take her arm, and begin to tug her out of her limo. She must weigh all of eighty pounds, including her jewels.

"Always look at their hands."

This is one of the first pieces of advice I had been given upon my arrival at Tate by my friend and personal mentor, Cookie Henderson, who I have known for years and who has worked forever as a fund-raiser at a local university. I call Cookie "The Kirby," because she has sucked up more money and dirt than anyone in the history of education. "The facelift scars can be hidden, my dear, the hair can be added, the lips puffed, but their hands always tell the truth," Cookie had told me.

As I take Mrs. Van Cleve's arm, I stare at her hands. Extending just beyond the eighteen carat gold Cartier cuff bracelet are the hands of a zombie.

"What a gentle-man," she says. "And I pause between that word for good reason."

She winks a fake eyelash at me, and I escort her—ever so slowly—into the reception area of our Alumni Hall, a massive building on our campus that looks like it is part Yale University and part Tara plantation. On the elevator ride up to the reception area, I make small talk about how lovely she looks—"Are you sure you're not celebrating your tenth reunion?"—and how incredibly academic Tate remains—"Twelve young ladies were accepted to the Ivies, and . . ." I stop for effect. Mrs. Van Cleve's donor file is drilled into my head, her life my late-night reading for the past week. I know more about her than her plastic surgeon—"and *three* young women will be attending Smith College next fall."

She beams.

I want to vomit.

Our routine for Alumnae Reunion guests is scripted and drilled into all staffers' heads. First, take their wraps, furs, handbags or purses, and swiftly deliver them to coat check, picking up their nametags on the way back.

Second, and most important, above all else, offer to get them a drink ASAP—repeating their order for clarity—without ever showing shock or concern about their future sobriety.

"A double Bushmills on the rocks? Certainly, Mrs. Van Cleve. Please wait here, I will return immediately."

Drink secured, you now place their nametag on their upper right chest—so it is not obscured when they shake hands—but *only* after garnering their approval. Despite the fact that nearly every woman's outfit is eerily similar, most Tate alumnae spend a fortune getting decked out for today's luncheon.

Bottom line: You *never* stick anything directly onto the outfit of a Tate alumna without asking first.

"Would it meet your approval, Mrs. Van Cleve, if I were to adhere your nametag to your blouse?"

"Let me help you, dah-ling," she winks again, guiding my hand up and over her breast three times before helping me slap it onto her chest.

"Let's just make sure it stays," she says, grabbing my hand and grinding it into her insanely firm ninety-three-year-old booby one more time.

She takes a chug of her whiskey and laughs heartily, leaning on the walker the chauffeur has just dispensed in front of her, lifting up the hem of her pink-fringed Chanel skirt to show the top of her support hose.

I look away quickly, for fear that I will be turned to stone. Nearly everyone in the room, I now notice, is wearing pink, even though it's a fall luncheon. I feel like I'm in that old Pepto-Bismol commercial, where the liquid runs down the front of the TV screen. Most women over sixty-five are wearing Chanel suits, a lot of jewelry, and rather tight faces, their foreheads now their scalps, their eyelids now their foreheads. Most look like very elegant but very surprised trout. Nearly every woman under sixty-five is wearing a pink, floral Lilly Pulitzer dress, as though they thought they might be attending the Kentucky Derby instead of a reunion event in September. Fashion sense isn't just a step behind the times at Tate and our city, it's simply frozen in time and trend.

I excuse myself for a moment, descend a small marble staircase that is directly behind us, and quickly return with an honor corsage, a tasteful, pink-hued orchid with a sprig of greenery, featuring a ribbon in Tate's colors as backing. These corsages were our staff's brilliant idea, a way of honoring all alumnae who were celebrating a reunion of fifty years or more. Tate alums crave recognition and love to be coddled: It's what their lives are all about.

We even had our honor corsages specially made by Petal Pushers—*the* flower boutique of high society in our city—with foam-wrapped clips, so they wouldn't leave a pin mark, much less a dent. I had even managed to incorporate pink to please Kitsy.

I thought I had all my bases covered.

But I incorrectly assume that Mrs. Van Cleve's approval for the nametag also means her approval for the honor corsage. I mistakenly forget that a ninety-three-year-old woman can't chug a double whiskey and still remember what she said five seconds earlier.

As I reach in to secure her corsage, she, without warning, raises up with her walker—like a wild horse that refuses to be saddled—and, with all the power and strength of a woman half her age and twice her weight, shoves me down the small staircase. I go down the stairs like a Slinky, a body part careening off each step, ultimately crashing into the legs of a tuxedoed violinist.

"Do you know how much this blouse costs?" Mrs. Van Cleve screams at me from five steps up, shaking her walker at me, still holding her whiskey, the previously flirty old lady now a diamond-encrusted Medusa. "What type of *unmarried . . . heathens* are working at *my* school today?"

With that, the violinist simply steps over my crumpled body and continues playing, his bow not missing a stroke of "Swan Lake." For just a second, the music fills my head, and I think, *I didn't fall. No. I glided to this spot on gilded wings, floated here like a prima ballerina.*

But then I see my legs, my ass, and they're not where they should be. Then I realize it's not music filling my head, it's probably blood.

Though I want to cry, to dig my way through this marble to the center of the earth so I can hide for eternity, or at least until I can stand on my own, I have to give it to the old bitch. She is clever. And dramatic, in a drunken Barbara Stanwyck meets Bette Davis sort of way. And I'm at least thankful I didn't fall on my own, which I typically do once a week at Tate, tripping down just-waxed marble staircases or sliding across a freshly scrubbed terrazzo floor.

Many nice, caring women rush to my side, check to see if I am OK, and they reaffirm my suspicions, albeit a bit too late: Yes, she is old; yes, she has always been mean; and, yes, she can be prone to such outbursts, especially when she has a drink.

I manage to lift my neck and look up the landing to see that Kitsy is glaring at me. Her eyes are shining like the aquamarine birthstone I had in my high school class ring, the one I polished every single night. Though Kitsy is *technically* not my boss, it is universally understood that, theoretically, she is everyone's boss.

Technically, my boss is a man named Doty, who is currently schmoozing with Kitsy. Doty has convinced me, despite the scientific evidence, that it *is* possible for a man to go through "the change of life." Doty is our ever-menopausal head of academic affairs, who, though not even part of our office, oversees seemingly every aspect of the school, including homework. In the sea of tan bodies and pink dresses, Doty is pale and wearing some sort of bizarre, Greek-inspired all-white pantsuit that makes him look like a chubby ghost. White, unfortunately, is Doty's iconic fashion statement, which is like saying Bjork's swan dress at the Oscars was sheer brilliance. At least Doty is easy to pick out at Tate functions: a man in white who resembles a gender-bending Florence Nightingale.

Doty is the only person in the entire crowd who is eating; he is shoveling spring rolls and petit fours down his throat like he's been shipwrecked for months. Or like he died and his very hungry spirit returned to haunt fast food restaurants and buffet lines.

Kitsy stands, extricating herself from Doty—who doesn't seem to have noticed that I am lying comatose on the ground; *Did he even see me?*—and moves elegantly toward my crumpled body. I watch her calves flex and muscle as she descends the stairs, I watch the light flash and glint off her subtly stunning array of diamonds. She is over me now, casting a shadow, and I think she is going to help me up. She is a mother. She has given birth. Mothers have that natural instinct to help those in need, right?

The nice group of older alumnae stooping over me quickly scatter upon her arrival, like quail following a gunshot, and I look up expectantly, even manage to reach out my hand to her, frowning in pain, but she only traces a smile across her face with her perfectly manicured index finger, like she's carving a face into a jack-o'-lantern with a sharp knife. "Get up! Now!" she mouths. I smile, out of requirement, ignoring my pain, my humiliation, and then, just like the violinist, Kitsy steps over my body.

She is even wearing pink panties.

Suddenly, I remember the afternoon I was eight years old and slid on an errant French fry at a restaurant in my rural childhood hometown. My plate flew like a food-filled Frisbee into the head of an old man whose teeth popped out into his grits. I remember my Grandma Shipman helping me onto my feet and saying, "Wee-Pooh, everyone falls. The beauty lies in the grace with which you get back on your feet."

And so, some three decades later, without my grandma there to help me up and make me feel better, without any real idea of where I'm going, I do just that.

I push myself off the floor with as much dignity as I can muster. Oddly, no one is acting like anything is wrong, like a man did not just fly through the air, screaming out in midflight like a teenaged girl who has just seen Leonardo DiCaprio, his head careening off the floor, a dead woman berating him from above.

I see a fellow staff member look at me from across the marbled foyer, shrug, and smile, before offering a dead woman in diamonds and fur a glass of champagne.

I stare at the scene for a moment; I actually see two scenes, double images of a corpse sipping something bubbly.

"Wade! Wade! Mrs. Jacobs is here," another staffer whispers in my ear, as I unsteadily make my way back to the nametag table. "You look woozy. Are you OK?"

I nod unconvincingly and lean against the nametag table for support. I could use a drink myself. And an ice bag. My coworker reaches over and knocks a half-eaten crab cake off my back, and then tries to peer into my glassy eyes.

"Wade! Are you sure you're OK? Mrs. Jacobs is waiting!"

I walk outside our Alumni Hall, the bright sun making my head throb even worse.

"It's lovely to see you again, Mrs. Jacobs," I say, helping a ninety-three-year-old woman who looks like Jackie Collins out of her limo.

As I reach for her arm, I instinctively look at her hands, hearing Cookie's advice in my head, trying nonchalantly to ignore her giant canary diamond ring, which costs more than I will make in five years combined.

Mrs. Jacobs' hands look like the Cryptkeeper's. With better nails, of course.

I don't, however, have the nerve right now to look at my own hands. I can feel them shaking, the cracks in my unpenetrable bee-keeping armor finally beginning to show.

It is at this moment, this crucial yet humiliating juncture in my life, in my "career," that I hear the questions exploding in my head, the ones that are pounding even louder than my jostled brain fluid, my irregular heartbeat; the questions I have been too scared to ask myself until now:

What am I doing with my life?
How the hell did I get here?
And why in the hell would I want to stay?

Name That Tune!

It is the spring of 1976, the Bicentennial in the Buckle of the Bible Belt. I am eleven, and our country grade school class is holding an inappropriately named Talent Contest in our "auditorium," which resembles a bus barn and consists of a basketball court on one side and our makeshift "stage" on the other. Our stage is a sloping, unfinished plywood platform that looks like the porch on a condemned house: gym equipment, tires, and bus parts stick out from underneath it.

I take the stage in a grape corduroy suit, the wings of my feathered hair making my head look as if it just might, suddenly, take flight. I grab the old mic, which emits an ear-piercing reverb, and squeak a hearty "Hello!" to the smattering of parents and grandparents who truly believe their children have talent, truly believe their hillbilly spawn can snatch the gold trophy I see sitting off to my right out of my well-lotioned hands.

I open my mouth and begin to sing a cappella. I am good. I know I am good. The song sounds exactly like it does when I hear it sung on the AM country radio station, Ozarks Country.

"Delta Dawn, what's that flower you have on?
Could it be a faded rose from days gone by?"

I try to connect with the audience, but I can see old men in overalls and women in aprons begin to snicker behind cowboy hats. Still, I finish, strong and proud, undeterred.

When the winners are announced, I am not among the names called. In fact, I walk away with nada, losing to a boy and girl who performed a bluegrass medley, the boy's fiddle sounding like a cat that had been set on fire, the girl's voice sounding like a cat that had been set on fire. It didn't matter how much talent they lacked, because they had ended with a medley of "God Bless America" and "Stars and Stripes Forever." I had mistakenly forgotten to honor our nation on its bicentennial.

"At least I can carry a tune!" I remember saying, after the contest.

"I think it was more about song choice," a friend had said, sounding a lot like Paula Abdul in pre–American Idol days. " 'Delta Dawn' . . . sung by a boy . . . holding a faded rose. It might have been a bit too much for this crowd."

Two weeks later, I am invited to the popular, luminescent Daphne DeWitt's birthday party. I am never invited to anything and am beyond thrilled, staying awake every night, picturing every last nuance of the party in my mind.

Daphne is Farrah blond, with silvery braces and perky boobies. She always smells like root beer; her mother looks like Susan Anton and sells Avon. I arrive at Daphne's party, thinking I have made it to the upper echelon of Ozarks society. In reality, I have been asked as a joke, to perform an encore of "Delta Dawn" for the amusement of Daphne, her mother, and their friends. I do as expected, thankful to simply be invited to the party of the spring. Following my performance, I schmooze the crowd, complimenting all the girls and their mothers, doing whatever I need to do in order to stay in this exhalted circle of popularity. I make Daphne laugh, and I bring

Susan Anton ice-cold glasses of Tickle Pink wine from the brand new almond-colored refrigerator that sits in the harvest gold kitchen of her brand new split-level. Her mom calls me "Dough-Boy" and tries to tickle my tummy and make me giggle like Poppin' Fresh.

I do as expected.

I Notice How Dirty
the Tile Is

The Monday following Reunion weekend, I come to work angry and bruised, my carefully crafted resignation letter folded in my hand. I enter filled with a sense of high drama, ready to walk into Doty's office, turn over his conference table, and throw my white letter in his pale face.

Instead, I discover a beautifully gift-wrapped box waiting for me in front of my office door.

I rip the box open, like a kid at Christmas, standing in the hallway. I smile. It is a new, black Kenneth Cole belt—the kind where the pretty silver buckle attaches seamlessly to the belt. It is from Kitsy. I am, sadly, impressed, considering my parents just stopped buying me Dockers, Wranglers, or overalls for Christmas. I dig deeper into the box. New sunglasses! Hip little shades that fit perfectly on my head and make me look like Jude Law. The pink note attached to the box states, "You did an amazing job with Reunion . . . despite that nasty 'accident.' We are going to make a great Tate team. FYI . . . These will look better with your Kenneth Cole suits."

Kitsy is abusive, she is passive-aggressive, and she is self-serving, but she is pretty, and I think she likes me. She really, really likes me. And, damn, if she doesn't have good taste.

I carry the belt and sunglasses into my office. My outlook is quickly and significantly brighter. I tuck my resignation letter into my pocket. Still, an assistant in the office smiles nervously at me, giving me the backwards eye roll, meaning someone is waiting in my office. This assistant spent so much of her childhood in Bible school and church, she is an expert at nonverbal communication. I know when she has to pee, when I need to be quiet in a meeting, when she has a new pen waiting at the ready for me because my current one is going to run dry . . . now.

I walk into my office to find an upset mommy waiting for me. This is not anything new, mind you, but it certainly has a different twist than the typical parents I find waiting or the typical crises I am used to hearing—not enough "good" coffee at the meeting, or the muffins were "reduced fat," not "low fat." In situations like this, my words usually flow freely, like honey into Winnie the Pooh's mouth.

Not today.

Because what exactly do I say to an African-American mother, a new parent at Tate, who confidentially tells me and no one else that, as she and her entire family drove onto campus for an event— dressed to the nines and ready to have the time of their lives—she was stopped by two of our volunteers—whom I believe to be our very worst M²s—and informed that parking for the catering staff was located behind the shed? And, she tells me, that they would probably have their pay docked for not wearing their uniforms and name badges?

I say nothing to her because I am weak and a coward.

I say nothing—though I know I should, because I never do— because I can hide. I am a white man. I can hide that I'm gay. She can't hide the fact that she's black. She doesn't need to know that I feel ostracized every single day, that her pain is my pain. Right?

I say nothing.

The mother is weeping uncontrollably in a stunning purple pantsuit, while her husband stands behind her, rubbing her shoulders. Her daughter, a new student at Tate, sits shell-shocked in an office chair, staring at her shiny shoes, the blue and yellow balls at the ends of her braids spinning like confused planets around her head. The girl's grandmother rocks back and forth in an adjoining wooden chair, nervously smoothing her gray hair and pulling Kleenex from her purse, saying, "Nothing's changed. Nothing will ever change."

My God. What has she seen in her life? And what are we doing to make things better?

I know this is the reason God has put me here, right now, to help at times like this. This is real life education, what our students need to learn about: the discrimination that surrounds them every day; the hardships that envelope our city and our world; the pain that sits percolating just over these manicured hedges; the prejudice that can often boil on their very own campus.

We talk about being an "inclusive" and "welcoming" community every day at Tate, and we try hard to change our history, to change our hallways, to change children's lives. We are winning, one day at a time, but change is still difficult and slow to come, no matter how hard we try. It's easier to talk sometimes than to listen. That's just too uncomfortable. That's why people often come to me, because I am the one who can listen and nod and soothe.

The mother looks at me, forcing herself to stop sobbing. "How could this happen?" she asks. "Does this happen all the time here?"

She is confused, confounded, her fury and outrage momentarily muted by her shock and surprise. I want to help her, to tell her the truth, my truth, the way it is here, that there are some very good people working very hard to change things, but I think it's going to take a long time, a very long time.

I start to tell her all of this, but the truth gets locked in my throat, and I begin to choke.

"Are you OK?" she asks.

And I nod, although I'm not, excusing myself to the men's room, where I sit on the floor next to the toilet, a sad man wearing a nice suit, still clutching a stylish belt and ritzy sunglasses, covering the sound of his cries of helplessness and rage and sadness and weakness by constantly flushing.

I return to the family, composed, and speak. But I do not speak the truth. Rather, I tell them their situation is an anomaly, that the two women who spoke to them were from a temporary agency, that this *never* happens at Tate. I apologize and I hug and I kiss mom and grandma on the cheek. I do my job. I lie. All for some pretty presents and the chance to be liked by someone I don't even respect. Soon, this family will have a wonderful experience at the school, be embraced and valued and loved, be incredible members of the community. But right now, I don't know that.

So, I go home that night and tell my partner, Gary, about my day, about this family.

"You have to leave," he says. "I thought you were going to quit."

"I can't just quit. That's not what sane people do. And I want to help," I reply. "I need to help. One day I will. I know I will, and that makes all of this tolerable."

"You're sad. And that makes me sad," Gary tells me before we go to sleep. As he reaches over to turn off the bedside lamp, Gary leans in and whispers, "You can't save the world until you save yourself."

That night I dream I am onstage at Tate's auditorium. I walk to the microphone and open my mouth. I plan to tell everyone that I am gay, that we all need to work together, that we shouldn't be mean to each other. "We're a school, for God's sake!" I want to say. But when I reach the mic, I look over to the side of the stage, where I see Kitsy pull a lever in the shape of a trophy. The floor under my feet disappears, and I drop into the sky, where I begin to float, fly.

"Hey, everyone! I can fly!" I try and scream out. But the only thing that comes out of my mouth is:

"Delta Dawn, what's that flower you have on?"

Where's the Girl with the Mole?

I'm on my way to meet Kitsy in carpool. She just called me this afternoon to ask if I could possibly get her favorite author, Candace Bushnell, to stop by Tate's Book Fair this Friday.

"Oh, my God, can you imagine? It shouldn't be that hard to schedule, right? We must do it—we'll be heroes. Everyone I know just adores her. Hurry! TTFN!"

I already picture myself dressing in a Prada miniskirt, padded bra, and blond wig, signing copies of *Sex and the City* and *Four Blondes* as my Lee Press On Nails fall into the pages.

I hurriedly lunge-walk my way along the brick sidewalk—my back, knees, and head still aching from my Reunion fall—silently yoga chanting.

As I walk, I look around our campus—thinking of Kitsy and Candace Bushnell—and take in the boys and girls cavorting on the expanse of green lawn that fronts our campus, at the teachers talking with mommies. And it hits me: Nearly everyone at Tate Academy is pretty.

This whole scene looks so innocent, really, like the backdrop for one of those after-school specials I watched in the late seventies where Robby Benson, Helen Hunt, and all the rich, mean kids learn a very important lesson from the poor boy with Down's syndrome.

But that's entertainment. This is real life. There's a big difference. But also a huge similarity. Most everyone on our set is gorgeous, too, just like in Hollywood.

Why don't we take more students who are unattractive, or fat, or hire more faculty members who, at least, have stringy hair? I know that we do, that this is an exaggeration, but they are mostly hidden, staff members behind cubicle walls, or bodyless voices over the phone. I know; I used to hide, too. But, for the most part, the majority here seem fit, firm, and fantastic, which infuses me with jealousy, envy, and amazement.

On my way to meet Kitsy, I think about this. It is disconcerting to me in a don't-even-think-about-it-or-you'll-go-nuts sort of way, one of those things you obsess over if you give in to it, like why asparagus makes your pee stink.

As I quickly walk, my mind adrift, I run smack dab into the Barbies, the title that four of the most popular, most beautiful girls have named their clique. I slow and smile nervously at them. Even as an adult, I get panicked, sweaty, passing the Barbies. I actually wet my lips and try to walk with as much confidence as I can muster, like a transgendered Heidi Klum.

I'm a grown man. Can you imagine being a *little* girl who's not a Barbie?

The Barbies all wear something pink, nearly every day. It might be a hair ribbon, or belt, or sweater, or scarf, but pink is their calling card. Along, of course, with being intimidating. I never hear much of what the Barbies say, since the majority of their conversations are Shakespearian stage whispers into pierced ears followed by giggles and "Oh, my Gods!" But I catch enough from the few words I am able to overhear. Who knew that such plain, dull English words could carry so much hidden meaning?

"Look at *those* shoes!"

"Look at her *hair!*"

"Where'd she get *that* purse?"

"OH.

"MY.

"GOD!"

Today, the Barbies are wearing pink cashmere turtlenecks and shimmery pink scarves with no coats. The sun is backlighting them, their white blonde hair, their perfect bone structure, their trendy clothes. They seem to know instinctively that they should always stand this way, in this direction, with their shoulders back and hips slung forward, for maximum effect.

They look like replicas of their very pretty moms, who are also chatting in a foursome just a few feet away. These Mean Mommies are all friends of Kitsy's, though their daughters are much older. I see them all chatting in the middle of carpool. The Barbies' M^2s already have their routine down for the year: They abandon their SUVs every single morning and afternoon before carpool and take a stand on the old brick sidewalk that curves along the cobblestone carpool lanes. They ogle the passing mommies, whispering and pointing and giggling just like their daughters, just like Joan Rivers on the red carpet.

"Look at *those* shoes!"

"Look at her *hair!*"

"Where'd she get *that* purse?"

"OH.

"MY.

"GOD!"

These are the Mean Mommies with whom I often work. They are usually the Karl Roves of Tate, the ones—though they comprise just a fraction of all the magnificent moms here—who tend to call the shots, rule the roost, lord over this educational feifdom like mean queens.

These mommies are usually the prettiest mommies, the "bore-dest" mommies—they are the former corporate CEOs and CFOs, the doctors, lawyers, and Indian chiefs, who married well, were successful, then had children and, at their husbands' requests, no longer work. That's our city's way. Still, their mommy motors hum along, fueled by caffeine and an unquenching desire to still be in charge of something, anything—book fairs, scrapbooking, progressive dinners, people's lives—and so they simply transfer their manic energy to Tate, to me.

"Helicopter parent" is the national buzzword that is pinned on these moms who hang around schools across the country all day long, "volunteering" at their children's schools, "donating their time and money" to the places they love, "being actively involved" in their children's lives. Most helicopter parents here do great things and great work, but, in all honesty, my few M^2s are simply meddling, not just hovering like a helicopter but actually going ahead and landing on the rooftop, rappelling into my office, and staying for the day. Once inside, they have the ability to run the school the way they see fit, to charge faculty and staff, like well-heeled bulls, ready to attack because their sons weren't named starters on the varsity team, or because their daughters didn't make the cheerleading squad. And they don't stop until they have gored their instigators in the heart.

This describes the M^2s of the Barbies, who have all been friends since starting in junior kindergarten together at Tate. I secretly call the Barbies' mommies the "Pink Ice Barbies," not only because each M^2 looks like an older version of her daughter but also because they look like the classic Pink Ice Barbie doll, the one I secretly bought and hid under my bed, the version where Barbie sports a shellacked blond updo or shimmery mass of gorgeous tendrils along with a traffic-stopping pink outfit.

Today, each Pink Ice Barbie M^2 is wearing a Lilly Pulitzer shift.

They are oohing and aahing over each other's pink dresses, enchanted, I hope, more by the designer's chosen names for their individual patterns—"Balloon Race," "Derby Days," "Southern Belle," and "Millionaires' Row"—than the actual designs, all of which look like ugly baby quilts.

Standing here, the Barbies and Pink Ice Barbies are like identical sets of quads. It looks as though fission has just taken place in a snotty little blond cell, each part producing a version that is pinker, tinier, and tanner than the previous.

The Pink Ice Barbies all live on the same cul-de-sac, and they all have eerily similar nicknames, which they bestowed on one other in grade school: Riffie, Miffie, Tiffie, and Spiffie. The Pink Ice Barbies all married perfect Tate Ken dolls who fit the Mean Mommy Husband stereotype.

All M^2 husbands, by the way, fit my Mean Mommy Husband stereotype to a tee. It's the standard to which all wealthy men in our city must conform. Without a doubt, a Mean Mommy Husband will always be one of the following things, usually in this descending order of societal importance: doctor (obscure specialty area); doctor (surgical); doctor (general practice); doctor (ophthalmologist); doctor (orthodontist); doctor (dentist); doctor (vet); attorney; engineer; banker; stockbroker; investor.

I had incorrectly assumed at first that Riffie was the designated leader of the Pink Ice Barbies—like Stockard Channing was the leader of the Pink Ladies in *Grease*—simply because she was a quarter inch taller than the others, or that she was a bit thinner, or that her voice was a bit squeakier. I have come to realize, however, that it's really because her husband is at the top of the corporate food chain, and her daughter is a "Cable Kid," a model-slash-actress who sings and dances on our local cable station and makes appearances at malls and pet food stores around town, singing "You Ain't Nothin'

But a Hound Dog" at PetSmart in front of admiring grandmothers and stray dogs.

The Pink Ice Barbies stand here at carpool staring down trespassers, those who do not live up to the standard which they have set.

I am certain I don't meet their standard. And I am not wearing pink today.

My heart races as I approach the Barbies and their M²s. I smile brightly again at the girls, at their mothers—*like me, like me*—but they don't smile back, because they don't have to.

The matching quartets simply turn in to each other and whisper as I pass. I clamp my eyes shut and wait for the giggles, which come—they always come—like machine gun fire.

And the bullets connect.

Still, I wet my lips and continue walking. I have to convince Kitsy that Candace Bushnell is on a book tour in Fiji.

It works, but Kitsy is none too pleased to attend a Book Fair that features only books.

Honey, Can You Stop at the Dry Cleaner's?

The first time I met Kitsy Ludington I didn't even know it. All I knew was that she had the look of someone I should know, the aura of a movie star who had decided to hide away in our city for a few days to escape the paparazzi, like Reese Witherspoon in Des Moines.

I had stopped at the dry cleaner, the nice one that charges ten dollars to starch a shirt, where I followed a tan, thin, beautiful blond woman wearing iridescent pink into the shop. She was carrying a little dog that I at first mistakenly thought was the end of a fox stole.

"I can't believe your delivery trucks are all down?" this magical figure told the dry cleaner, speaking in the mystical dialect I would later term the question-command. "Can you even comprehend the inconvenience this has created? This will change." He nodded, as though he knew the inconceivable pain he had caused her, and quickly scampered away to retrieve her dry cleaning. I remember thinking, "My God! Who *is* this woman?" along with, "You mean her dry cleaning isn't on the spinning rack like mine?"

As she picked up a fur from winter storage, along with a pink suit and pink-and-green jacket, the bedazzled dry cleaner somehow summoned the courage to ask her *the question*.

"The question" in our city is the one that every local asks, in every part of the city, whether they know you or not. It is the question you are asked at parties and grocery stores, in movie lines and at gas stations, by random strangers. It is asked because you can then be immediately categorized. Despite our city's size and diversity, it just takes this one simple question to define us, to sum up our collective insecurity, the insecurities of our poorest and wealthiest citizens.

The question is: "Where did you go to high school?"

Not college, not "Where do you work?" or "What do you do?" but rather, what high school did you attend.

Being fairly new to the city, I had already learned about the power and mystique our local schools carried. There is a school on every neighborhood corner, on every city block, on every clear-cut, treeless field in every brand new, outlying suburb: There are Catholic schools for girls and Catholic schools for boys, schools for Methodists and Christian Scientists, there are ancient, brick city schools in decaying neighborhoods, and mammoth new high schools that look like prefabricated churches for five thousand worshipers. There are small colleges and big universities, too, dotting the city.

Still, I didn't yet realize that there was really only one acceptable answer here, one school—public or private, religious or nonsectarian, old or new—that made strangers look at you with envy and desire, like you were a celebrity, like *you* were Reese Witherspoon.

The woman in pink, holding her pink dry cleaning and pink-clad dog, stated proudly, as though she were revealing the Oscar winner for Best Actress: "Tate Academy." And then the funniest thing happened: The tiny dry cleaner bowed in the woman's direction, like she was royalty, like he had confused this miniature blonde for a wig-bedecked Prince Charles.

I knew right then and there. My destiny was written on the wall, just like the cost for "heavy starch." I would work at Tate Academy. I would be part of the in-group for once in my life.

What I didn't know at the time were the following three things: That this pink woman would become my inspiration and my nightmare; that I should have been careful for what I wished; and that the dry cleaner was much smarter than I, because he already knew to bow down to Kitsy Ludington.

Kitsy Plants a Garden

Kitsy Ludington walks at the speed of light. Watching her streak across campus this late September morning is like watching a cheetah go after an antelope on the Nature Channel.

And I'm a runner, a fast runner, yet somehow it's impossible for me to keep up with this pink blur in raffia mules.

"Don't fall!" Kitsy yells at me, laughing, bringing up my Reunion debacle once again like it's a little joke between two old friends. "My God, that was so embarrassing, wasn't it? I was humiliated for you. I mean, my daughter learned to walk at ten months, and she hasn't had any trouble staying upright since."

Who talks to people like this? Especially someone they barely know?

But I already know that when Kitsy speaks to others, her purpose is single-minded. It isn't simply to puncture their self-esteem, to insert a pin into a balloon and watch it slowly float back to earth—an ego adjustment we all need on occasion—but rather to deflate their entire soul, like the *Hindenburg*, to send their beings crashing to the ground in flames.

"It was an unfortunate accident," I say, wondering why I'm covering for the old broad who I feel purposely shoved me down a staircase. Do I say what's on my mind? No. I compromise, as usual, finding a polite middle ground. "Actually, I think I was pushed," I say. "It *may* have been an accident, she may have stumbled into me, but I think I was pushed. It all happened so quickly."

Kitsy stops and lasers in on me with those eyes, which match the crisp blue fall sky perfectly today.

"I saw you go down for manhandling an old woman," Kitsy chortles in her I'm-laughing-at-you-not-with-you way. "Let's just say you 'slipped,' OK?"

I start to say, "No! That's not OK," but I don't, partly because I don't have the guts and partly because Kitsy is now yelling, "*Antirrhinum majus!*"

"What?" I ask. "What are you saying?"

"Snapdragon! *Antirrhinum majus* is snapdragon. Who doesn't know that?"

Kitsy and I are surveying Tate's campus in advance of the Garden Auxiliary's fall planting. I am walking around with a notepad, accompanying her, jotting down the Latin names of the plants Kitsy calls out. I feel like the illegitimate son of Socrates and P. Allen Smith.

The goal of our Garden Auxiliary is twofold: First, to help our overworked grounds staff, who are swamped with caring for over two hundred acres of land; and, second, to help underwrite the cost of sprucing up the campus with fall plantings in advance of the endless array of upcoming autumn activities.

Today, however, is really just a ploy for Kitsy to do her own fall yard cleanup. We have had supporters pull this trick before; these are the types of efforts a fund-raiser like Cookie Henderson usually handles, since they are considered gifts in kind, but Kitsy's walk-through has been handed off to me.

Kitsy's goal today is to survey our campus and then have her landscaping service dig up plants she no longer likes or wants and "donate" them to Tate. This strategy not only lets her make a gift in kind to Tate instead of an actual cash gift—earning her credit in the Annual Report without really giving a penny of support this year—but I have been told it also serves as a nice little tax write-off.

Her need to do this baffles me. I don't understand how this tiny tax break can even help her.

Kitsy Ludington and her husband made their money the old-fashioned way: They inherited it.

Still, Kitsy and her husband leveraged their inheritances into even more money. They began by selling a stylish item at a lower cost to the common folk, slowly building their business, before finally selling it to a corporate conglomerate for one of those sums of money that makes you dizzy because there are so many zeroes.

I try to make small talk with Kitsy, and ask about her former business, how she ever came up with such an incredible concept.

She stops again and stares at me.

"What an interesting question," she says. "I was bored and shopping in a mall one day. I looked around and thought, 'Ugly people need to feel pretty sometimes, too.' That's how it came to me."

I am staring at Kitsy, nodding in agreement, like she is totally serious.

And she is. She is telling me this in an enlightened sort of way, almost as if she is telling me how she found God.

I continue to nod, wondering—with Kitsy's Up with People attitude—how Tate had ever deemed her worthy of multiple leadership roles.

But I know just by looking at her. She has a multimillion-dollar presence, a multimillion-dollar smile, when she cares to use it. Kitsy looks perfect—always looks perfect—in her endless supply of pink Lilly Pulitzer suits, skirts, pants, and jackets, double strands of freshwater pearls, subtly stunning diamonds flashing on her earlobes, fingers, and wrists, tan but not too tan, and with her sleek blond bob so heavily hair-sprayed that it wouldn't move in a centrifuge. Even today, looking casual in a pink, sleeveless Lilly golf polo and pink-ribbon-cuffed capris, she is perfect.

And it is her presence, her perfection, that makes my doubts disintegrate, makes me feel as though she is doing something worthwhile for Tate.

On one hand, the good one, I tell myself, she is donating plants that she thinks will complement the landscape or the architecture of our campus. Just not this year. On the other hand, the bad one, she's having me serve as her horticultural secretary, so this list can be given not only to her landscaping service but also to her accountant, I think.

"Tagetes patula!" she shouts, shaking me from my thoughts.

I wait.

Yes, I have to ask.

"What?"

"French marigold!"

But of course.

Later in the month, when the other moms on the Garden Auxiliary come to plant, I am sadistically amused to see their reactions when they are approached not by parent president and leader Kitsy Ludington but by Raul and Hector from her lawncare service, explaining, as best they can, that they have been sent to help by "Señora Kitsy" who is "too busy to be here."

"She say sorry," they tell us, before unloading their truck with hundreds of wilted, dying summer annuals that won't even make it through October.

Kitsy Orders the "You Pick Two"

Kitsy has a play date.

Early each fall, Tate Academy encourages its legacy families to link with newly enrolled families, so, as I like to say, "a deep and lasting connection can be made," "one that will last a lifetime," "one that will grow from a relationship based in mentoring to one based in friendship."

Kitsy calls this a play date. Kind of like a cat would call batting a mouse around a play date.

The intention of Tate, of most private schools, with this worthwhile endeavor is to help new private school families learn the ropes from those who have been around the block, the way veterans help rookies in football camp. For new students, this means getting help organizing their binders from current students, or talking about the right extracurriculars in which to get involved; for new parents, this should mean learning about which student organizational and study habits work best, or discussing with current parents how to get involved at Tate. It means, simply, being a friend, a role that most of our parents embrace.

For just *one* person, however, this means identifying which brand of new mommies are OK to socialize with and which ones should be ignored and isolated. The mommy with whom Kitsy has been paired—fresh from the South—falls immediately into the "ignore/isolate" category.

I have already met this mother numerous times. She is wonderfully refreshing—humorous, smart, self-deprecating—especially for our school community, for our city. She is doughy and drawly, like the Food Network's Paula Deen. She is a former teacher who understands what teachers go through, who respects their difficult jobs, who sees herself as a partner with Tate's faculty and administration, not simply as an adversary, in the education of her child.

These are big no-nos in Kitsy's world, where everyone is only deemed worthy if they are super smug and self-important and in full makeup at all times. In this world, no mother worth her salt would dare wear a sweatshirt to carpool; discussing parent-teacher partnerships, thus, equates heresy.

Naturally, Kitsy immediately summons me to carpool this afternoon to inform me that her play date did not go well. She tells me that the woman invited her over to her house and cooked for her. Made the entire meal *herself*. "Cooked for me, can you imagine such a thing?" she asks me through a crack in the passenger window. "Who has the time to do that? Who *wants* to do that? That's why I have my Clementine. Anyway, her whole house smelled like roast and onions. And she was wearing an apron!"

LulaBelle yodels in horror at her owner's plight and tone, and I swivel my head, like this is the most horrific thing I have ever heard in my life, like the woman had greeted Kitsy at the door and peed on the floor.

"I refused to eat, of course," she tells me. "She served some sort of cream soup and some sort of sandwich with meat."

LulaBelle continues to yodel, and I continue to swivel my head, picturing the woman offering Kitsy a bowl of gruel and a rat between two slices of Wonder.

"And she told me her goal is to change parent perspectives about faculty. She wants to promote a healthy parent partnership, where we all work together in the best interests of the child. It all just sounded so very odd."

I am wide-eyed in horror, imagining Paula Deen lighting candles and then beheading either a goat, or LulaBelle, in front of Kitsy.

"What kind of families are we accepting here? What is happening to this school? My school? This isn't *Atlanta* or *Dallas,* for God's sake. She was so . . . *Southern.* I plan to ask about this. Change is in the air, and change is not good."

Kitsy is shaking her head, and as she thumps the gas pedal of her Land Rover, my neck jerks sideways like a bobblehead's.

"I have to tell this to the girls," Kitsy says, her sunglass-cloaked head now pointed in the direction of the Pink Ice Barbies, who are hooting and hollering today on the sidewalk, while the younger Barbies paint each other's nails and look bored. "They will absolutely die. TTFN!" she yells. I release my fingers just in time and stare at my saved digits, wanting desperately to walk over to the Barbies, hold out my nails, and say, "Me next!"

Instead, I soon learn that while change may not be good, neither is directness. Kitsy will not approach anyone to discuss anything; many who are upset here never will. Rather, they will send anonymous letters or e-mails, which is what I will later be told has been done, that details how Tate is ignoring its legacy families. These letters—and there will be an infinite number about an infinite number of topics sent during my tenure—are always from an anonymous committee with an obscure and ever-changing name. I call this group "The Snipers," because they hide anonymously in the bushes and on rooftops, taking potshots at anyone that angers or upsets them: heads of divisions, faculty, administrators, food service. I always have the uncomfortable feeling—like everyone else at Tate— that a silver bullet is waiting for me, a silent, nervous finger waiting on the trigger.

Trick or Treat!

I am wet. Soaking wet. Lost dog in the rain wet.

And Kitsy doesn't even seem to notice that water is cascading down over my eyes and off my shoulders. I think she believes I am an inanimate object, like the bronze Zen water sculpture she has in her serenity garden, the "garden of peace," as she calls it, the place she has her gardener change constantly to keep things "fresh and interesting," the one for which she had her landscape architect build a curved bridge out of bentwood, so she could place it over her new fishpond. Being this wet, I can actually relate to those unfortunate fish, actually feel sorry for them. I can hear Kitsy telling the koi every morning, "I'm so disappointed in your growth rate." I can hear them saying, their mouths in a constant O, "Oh! What a bitch!"

She has summoned me to morning carpool in this weather with the words, "I'm outside. TTFN!"

It is October. This month in our city is either sunny and warm or wet and cool. Today, it is wet and cool, which is why she has summoned me outside. To wear down my resistance. I know her tricks. In just a few minutes, the light sprinkles have turned into a downpour. I didn't bring an umbrella—make that would not bring my umbrella, since it's a hand-me-down from my mother, a nurse. My umbrella says, "Give a Nurse a Shot!" and features the name of a medical supply company that manufactures syringes. That just doesn't cut it at Tate. So I go au naturel.

Despite the fact I'm getting soaked, I am not invited inside the SUV, and no word about my well-being is uttered.

Rather, I am leaning into Kitsy's Land Rover, actually pulling myself into the passenger-side window like I'm trying not to fall from the window of a high-rise, and she keeps hitting the power window, knocking my arms off, so I fall back to earth. She scooches over and looks down at me through the window, smiling. "Please stay off my running board, Wade. It's for passenger use only," she says. Then she laughs. "*This* weather. It's raining cats *and* dogs, right, LulaBelle?"

LulaBelle barks her agreement. She is wearing a pink rain slicker.

"So here's my adorey-abuhl little idea, OK? You'd be a fool to think otherwise."

Kitsy suggests that since her husband will be out of town on business for Halloween (he is out of town constantly, by the way), I dress up as President Ronald Reagan to her Nancy for Halloween, and that we walk the Tate hallways together handing out candy.

I stare at her, blinking water out of my eyes, thinking she is pulling my rather wet leg. My leather shoes are disintegrating and pooled with water. I push my hair back; it is slick. I look like Pat Riley in the window's reflection.

"So? What do you think? It's perfect."

She's not joking.

This is the equivalent of asking Dr. Laura what she thinks about dressing in leather stirrups and marching in San Francisco's Pride Parade.

"So?"

I must be careful. I start to speak, but don't have a chance to get a word out.

Kitsy begins to raise her left hand, and it looks like she is going to lift her perfectly tanned index finger and scratch out my eyes with her perfectly manicured nail. Just for the hell of it. However, the weight of the diamond in her wedding ring, I believe, prevents her from lifting her fragile arm and doing this. Instead, she just points at me.

And then her face sprouts into an evil smile. "I'll have my assistant, Lilly, bring you an outfit. We have to do *something* to show our Tate spirit. The kids will just love it!" I stare at her. She has a lot of teeth. A lot of perfectly straight, glow-in-the-dark white porcelain veneers. Mostly, she has a lot of dry teeth, of which I am jealous.

I smile and blow water out of my face, a whale cresting on the ocean, and then nod, smiling loopily, like I've just had a lobotomy under a sprinkler. I stand and watch her drive away. *Of course, she would hire an assistant named Lilly.* I stay put, smiling and waving.

Kitsy could have suggested we come as Hitler and Mussolini, and I would have agreed by now.

Tomorrow, by this time, I will be sick. Physically, at first, with chills and a slight fever.

And then Kitsy's assistant Lilly, a perky, blond, newly minted Oberlin graduate who looks like Mandy Moore, will bring me at work hard, black plastic Reagan hair, big fake teeth, a glen plaid jacket, and a brown tie. I will get mentally sick then.

Lilly smells like her name. I smell like Vicks, which my assistant has loaned me. My assistant has everything in her bottom right desk drawer; it's like an underground Walgreens.

"Try on the hair, teeth, and tie, 'K?"

Everything Lilly says ends with a shortened, perky "OK?" She has picked up the question-command from Kitsy and given it her own MTV-inspired twist. *Bravo, Lilly.*

I stare at Lilly, as she attempts to transform me—a five-foot-seven-inch blond gay Democratic, Banana Republic devotee—into a tall, dark-haired, Republican cowboy. Lilly, I now notice, actually manages to make pink lipstick look good. *Bravo again, Lilly.*

"Oh my God! You can look now, 'K?"

She holds up a mirror that she plucks from her denim, Louis Vuitton–monogrammed handbag.

I look like a Pez dispenser.

"Spitting image," Lilly says. "Gotta go."

Lilly grabs her handbag and cotton candy colored cell phone, which is now trilling softly.

"Hi, Kitsy. Oh my God! He looks just like Ronnie."

I sit down shakily and catch my reflection in the computer screen of my computer. I try to adjust my plastic hair and teeth, thinking this slight tweaking might actually make a difference.

I want to laugh. But none of this is funny to me anymore.

Next week, thankfully too sick now to come to work and pass out mini-Snickers and tiny PayDays and baby Baby Ruths in fake hair, I stay in bed and imagine the scene: Children taunting me, the Barbies following me around asking if I am Beavis or Butthead, Kitsy laughing every time they ask me this, like they've coined the funniest catchphrase in the world, like "Wachoo talkin' 'bout, Willis?"

I later hear that Kitsy arrived—none too pleased to find I was out sick—looking exactly like Nancy Reagan, if Nancy Reagan had looked anything at all like Britney Spears. *I knew it. I knew she'd never dress up.* Nancy was also carrying the family dog—LulaBelle— who was sporting what I heard were faux vampire fangs and a pink cape.

Still, despite my cold, I will end up going out and getting drunk, very drunk, Halloween night and tell this story to all of my friends, tell them all my stories. They will say it sounds like fun, more fun than selling mutual funds or pharmaceuticals.

I will ask, after my third shot of Jaegermeister, if a mutual fund or a pill for erectile dysfunction has ever once made them go fetch a Starbucks.

"Well, have they?" I scream.

And then I will laugh like a donkey at my joke. A very drunk donkey.

Calendar Girl

My life at Tate follows a carefully orchestrated routine. Meetings, meetings, and more meetings.

Everything—schedules, kids, classes—runs by strict routine. This is a strange dichotomy in my life. I love routine, demand routine, for some aspects of my life, such as working out (always back-biceps Mondays, chest-triceps Tuesdays, shoulders-biceps Wednesdays, leg-triceps Fridays), but too much routine makes me nuts, too much organization makes me want to grind my teeth into Chiclets. I need a certain amount of creative freedom—to jot ideas on Post-its, to write nonsensical babble, to sketch my ideas for magazine covers—but my creative time is limited to a precious few moments each day.

Instead, my days here, like everyone's days here, are filled with endless, prescripted meetings. The not-so-subtle inference is: "We all must achieve as much as humanly possible." My daily calendar always looks like the guest list to an orgy in ancient Greece.

Carpool runs every day from roughly 7:20 to 8:00 in the morning, and 2:45 to 3:30 in the afternoon, times that make me wince as I pray for the phone not to ring.

Some Monday mornings, from 8:00 to 10:00 A.M., are devoted to "Monday Morning Muffins with Mommies," followed by at least two additional hours of gossip.

Tuesday mornings, we have staff meetings from 9:00 to 11:30 A.M.

Wednesday mornings I might babysit Miggie, followed by xeroxing for M²s.

Thursday mornings are our administration meetings, and Fridays are either devoted to taking photos at events like "Doughnuts & Dads" or huddling with Kitsy to plan the coming weekend and week. All of this leaves me precious little time for my "real" duties, like publishing alumni magazines, revamping the web site, handling media relations, and coordinating special events.

However—not counting carpool—Monday Morning Muffins with Mommies is my least favorite activity. It's up there alongside making out with women. Neither is really a great way to jump-start my new work week.

"Monday Morning Muffins with Mommies" is what I've secretly named this gossip session designed as a PR meeting. I named it this because it sounds like such a great time, doesn't it? It makes me feel good to think of the meeting this way, as a 1950s morning TV show, where June Lockhart and June Cleaver teach me how to bake and iron.

Today's Tate version is decidedly different, however. I stage it only for a select few of our M²s, to keep them intentionally separated from the good moms who can actually do things on their own. The M²s arrive looking like the cast of *Desperate Housewives,* all shiny and slick and perfect, carrying no-fat, no-whip Starbucks. And no one ever really *eats* an entire muffin; the food is here purely for show, kind of like me. Instead of school issues, I listen to the M²s discuss "important issues," like the renovations to their summer homes, thus ending my hope of getting any work done before noon. No matter what the conversation, Kitsy likes me to stay, so I can "soak up the ambience" and "connect with Tate's true constituents."

The Mean Mommies arrive at these VIP pow-wows like a swarm of killer bees, the women buzzing quickly and furiously around one another—hugging, kissing, and patting, without ever actually making any skin-to-skin contact—so that makeup, hair, clothes are never mussed.

If I think the sting of Kitsy, the single bee, alone, is painful, the fury of the entire hive is deadly.

On occasion, a new Tate mommy—a mother who moved from out of town, or isn't a legacy—will simply wander in and linger after the Morning Muffins with Mommies in order to try and join the elite swarm. But the M²s mostly treat her like a leper, as she waits patiently to be introduced, waits patiently for another mommy to approach her, waits even for the smallest opening to step in, but that never happens—and so she waits and waits and waits, before self-consciously backing up, like an innocent shopper who's wandered into a hold-up. The giggles of the Pink Ice Barbies, which always accompany a departure, seem, right now, sitting here, even worse than a spray of bullets. These are wounds that will never heal.

To remove myself from the horror at hand, I like to sit and watch Kitsy, the Pink Ice Barbies, and the other M²s pretend to eat. It is a wonderfully choreographed act. They cut finger foods into even tinier pieces, halving muffins with their knives, before dividing and subdividing them over and over again, like grains of salt, until only manageable crumbs remain. They pick them up with the skin of their forefinger and thumb, making sure the food never touches their perfectly manicured nails or their perfectly constructed lips. Glasses are wiped clean after nearly every drink, lipstick reapplied after nearly every sip. It is the dance of the self-obsessed.

When they are not pseudo-nibbling, they discuss the exact same conversational topics (delivered in highly energetic tones) every single meeting:

"How busy we are!"
"How great you (and she) look!"

"How smart and athletic your (and my) kids are!"

"The new chef at the country club!"

"The latest divorce!"

"Who's fat!"

"My latest vacation!"

"My latest summer home renovation in (please pick from the
    following: Aspen, Michigan, Naples, Door County)!"

"The latest charity ball!"

"The benefits of working out and only eating a Zone bar
    all day!"

My conversational topics have also been significantly reduced since starting at Tate. I can now say, in equally energetic tones:

"No, these are low-fat muffins, not reduced-fat."

"I agree. Egg Harbor has gotten too new-money."

"The new Baker Residence *is* hideous. I thought they only
    used stucco in Mexico."

On the nights following Monday Morning Muffins with Mommies I typically have the same dream: I have come to Tate as a gay man. Passing as a straight man. Who works only with women. And gets abused by mothers. I dream that I write a Broadway play called *The Stepford Wives: The Musical.* I cast the play first with Barbie dolls, but they just stand there, motionless, staring at me, so I hold auditions, telling the auditioning actresses to pretend to be robotic imitations of real women who have actual hearts and souls and minds of their own. No one gets my concept. I then try and pitch it to movie executives. "It's *Victor-Victoria* meets *The Nanny Diaries* meets *The Crying Game* meets *The Devil Wears Prada*." I do not get backing for my project.

I do, however, wake up and get ready to go in to work.

He's a What?

The hardest part of my Monday Morning Muffins with Mommies, however, comes when the M^2s, as I like to say, "make fun of the fags." It's part of a more universal discussion, of course, gays not being the sole agenda topic—like how Martha Stewart might discuss how to plant tulip bulbs, or make grapevine wreaths or homemade yogurt—but bashing gays occasionally gets air time.

My friends on the coasts cannot believe this when I relay my stories. They have become habituated to the acceptance that living in liberal, diverse, major metropolitan areas provides. They think acceptance of others who are different is normal, that *Will and Grace* and *Queer Eye* and gay-themed movies have made gays just another quilt square in the fabric of the United States.

But our city is not on the coasts. And being gay does not seem OK in this staunchly conservative, Republican, lily white suburb.

Recent presidential campaigns seem to have made it OK—actually, perfectly acceptable—for people to bash gays, to speak of them with complete and utter hatred and contempt, like they are killers or pedophiles, which I think the M^2s feel they are. I occasionally hear kids yell in the hallways, "That's so gay!" or "Stop it, fag!" or "Don't touch me, you big queer," and I have never *personally* heard anyone stop this, or point out that this type of hate language is not

OK. I know the school does not support this type of behavior yet somehow this passes muster while kids would never be allowed to walk the halls screaming, "Nigger!" or "Wop!" or "Towelhead!"

I guess what bothers me is that I don't stop it either, and I am really the walking embodiment of all their hatred, a wolf in sheep's clothing sent here to rip apart the moral fabric of this place.

So I simply walk by and listen in the halls, and then sit and listen with the M²s, who, when out of earshot of the good mommies, speak without embarrassment or fear of rebuke. They are in their safe zone.

"Two men marrying one another. Can you imagine? What is this world coming to?" asks a Mean Mommy who, in her thirties, has already been divorced numerous times, I have been told. She is now pregnant by a man thirty years her senior.

"It's a war for our children's morality," says a Pink Ice Barbie whose own Barbie has been caught twice this year, I've been told, in compromising positions with boys.

They talk as though I'm one of them. And it's hard to decide what aspect bothers me the most: their hatred; their self-serving smugness; their inability to see the irony in their own situations; the assumption that I think just like them; the complete impossibility to them that I might be gay. Or do they think I'm a woman?

Angry, I surprise myself by actually going to Doty and telling him how much this upsets me. I suggest that I be removed from this task and that someone else begin to help the group. "Perhaps a woman can be more effective," I suggest. Doty loves women's empowerment. I think it just means he has to do less work.

"I hear you," Doty says, "but this is one of your roles as PR Director. Perhaps you should set an agenda?"

For Muffins with Mommies? That's like having Charo debate Condoleezza Rice. After a while, you know she's going to stand behind the mic and go "Cuchi Coo!" when she's asked about foreign policy.

Suddenly, Doty's eyes bulge from his doughy face. "I've got it! Why don't you lead a diversity and sensitivity training session for that group? We've done it before with great success. It's perfect. You get to educate and they get to learn. It's a win-win!"

I want to tell Doty the only win-win is if I win a million dollars and get to drive away right now, that, in reality, it's a lose-lose, that I will be torn limb from limb, like a gay gladiator pitted against homophobic lions, and will still be expected to hand out low-fat muffins the next week at The Coliseum with just my torso.

I want to tell Doty that he shouldn't wear white, that he looks like some fashion-challenged Wimbledon champion, that I can't distinguish his pale hands from his white sleeves, his pale face from his light Miami Vice–esque jacket. I want to tell him that when he moves, he looks just like a ghost on an amusement park teacups ride.

But I don't.

"Great idea," I say.

Where's Jesse Jackson
When You Need Him?

I am not a diversity expert. Just because I'm gay does not necessarily mean I am well versed in the struggles of African-Americans or the history of Indian-Americans. Just because I have a weak Y chromosome doesn't necessarily mean I am fluent in women's issues.

I grew up in the middle of nowhere. I remember few, if any, minorities in our little town—no blacks, or Asians, or Hispanics. I don't even remember a Catholic. My town was mostly white, and mostly Baptist. The few Methodists in town were pretty much our minority population.

The first time I saw a black person was when we moved to Georgia for a brief time. The first day, as I accompanied my mom to the store, I asked a black woman if she were made of chocolate. "I want to taste you," I said. I will never forget the reaction of my mother or the woman, neither of whom showed embarrassment or humiliation or anger.

"We just moved from a small town," my mother explained. "I'm sorry."

The black woman stood in the store, next to an overflowing bin of Vidalia onions, bellowing in laughter. "Honey, it's OK. That's the sweetest thing I ever did hear," she said. And then she said something that resonates with me still today. "That's the innocence of a child talkin', not the hatred of adults."

I approach my meeting with the three or four attending M²s

with this in mind, trying to remember that a sliver of innocence surely remains in these mommies. It has to, because they have given birth, are raising children; they witness innocence waking up before them every day.

In preparation for my meeting, I had spoken with numerous minority and antidefamation organizations in town, seeking advice and counsel.

I am told to start with my own story from Georgia, to demonstrate that I am not perfect, that I am not preaching, that I am just like everyone else. We all make mistakes. We all continue to learn. This is, after all, a school. This is, after all, life.

I start my story, and instantly a tan, well-manicured hand goes up.

"Was this in Atlanta, Georgia?" one of the Pink Ice Barbies asks. I think it's Miffie. Or is it Spiffie?

"No, it was a very small town."

"Why would your family move to a small town in Georgia?" Riffie, the Pink Ice Barbie leader, asks incredulously.

"My father was transferred."

"Why would he move his family to a small town in Georgia?" she asks again, like a pink prosecuting attorney.

All around, these few M²s are nodding in agreement, aghast at the decision my family made decades ago. I'm thirty seconds in; how have I lost control already?

"I grew up in a small town. My family likes small towns."

Some M²s gasp out loud, as if an overweight woman has just walked into a gym in Spandex.

"Why are you living here then?" Riffie asks.

I use my surefire line. "Because I love our professional basketball team!"

It works. Everyone here worships the basketball team—it's city law. The mothers clap excitedly, like they're at a baby shower and the pregnant woman has just opened a pair of pink booties.

I start again, segueing into the stereotypes we all have about people who are different from us. I get another two minutes, before Kitsy interrupts.

"We all know what this is about, Wade, so let's just cut to the chase. I know that Tate wants to be more inclusive. So you can go back and say that we support the school's little diversity initiative as long as legacy families continue to get top consideration in admission policies. Agreed, ladies?"

The mommies again clap excitedly, except with considerably more enthusiasm, like the pregnant woman has just unwrapped an antique, hand-carved bassinet.

"Lunch at the Club. On me!" Kitsy announces, to more wild applause. And just like that, the diversity meeting is over, a pink swarm of bees buzzing out of the conference room.

On her way out, Kitsy stops me and says, "Nice try, Wade. That was so uncomfortable. It was like listening to NPR. Who put you up to that? What bullet won't you take for Tate?"

Who's at the Door?

The morning after my diversity debacle, Doty tells me during an emergency, closed-door meeting that I am not a good communicator.

"Didn't you ever take debate?" he asks. "You have to stand your ground, make your points. These women are not your friends. You work for me and the Board of Trustees, not a group of nosy mothers."

I nod, wishing I had Lilly's mirror right now, so Doty could take a good, hard look at himself.

In truth, Doty is a wannabe at the Academy, a Mean Mommy with a penis. He wants to be rich, he wants to be popular, he wants to be powerful, he wants to be a friend of the school's constituents, not an employee of the school. And that will forever cloud his judgment. You cannot be both. You will run on that wannbe popularity treadmill forever, just like a gerbil. I should know. I am still running, too.

"Work should fill your well, not people," he tells me in our meeting. "You can't please everyone. You should be here because you believe in what Tate is doing. You are here to serve, not mingle. Work is not about relationships. It's about the work. Hence, the name."

My head begins to go white, like his outfit, my anger making me dizzy. How can he not see himself? But then I think, *Is he right? Do I work for the wrong reasons?* People *are* my main motivation, not adding photos to a Web site, or drafting a press release for a school that's raised another record amount for its Annual Fund drive. Despite how the M²s treat me, I still look for the good in them. In everyone. Because I have seen—through my parents, through my friends—the incredible personal transformations that human beings can make in their lives. I have hope. Because I have always needed to have hope. To survive.

And then Doty says it. The line I despise, the one he says to staffers when he's not pleased with something we've done, when he wants to sound mildly threatening.

"Can you hear that? Can you? DING-DONG! DING-DONG! I think that's the doorbell. You might want to answer it, see who's there. It might be a different future coming to call."

Doty represents everything I hate about work, about bad bosses. Hypocrisy. Veiled threats. Demeaning attitude. Self-righteousness that hangs in the air like his bad cologne. I mean, who wears Old Spice any more? Doty is a Mean Mommy in sheep's clothing. Actually, not even wool. Just really bad polyester.

The saddest part is that I will see Doty after a lunch meeting today, trying to be a mover with all the movers and shakers. A VIP group of parents and alumni will be clustered together, laughing, whispering, sharing city secrets. Doty nods and smiles, inching closer to the action, his head ducked into his chest, his feet taking tiny little steps in his tiny little loafers toward the group—like Snoopy sneaking up on Lucy—until he is five feet away. Though he is so close to being a part of the group, he is never asked to join. The VIPs don't even know he is there. He is, literally and fashionably, a ghost.

Doty may have power at work, but he still doesn't have the power to change a damn thing in his own life.

But he does in mine. He tells me I need an organizational coach. "Perhaps being more organized would have improved your presentation yesterday."

The Dysfunctional
Dessert Table

Jesus.

It's already Tuesday, and time for our weekly staff meeting. I begin to stare at the clock on my computer for an hour every Tuesday morning before our meeting, dreading it. Our weekly staff meeting is me, Doty, and twelve women, the majority of whom I am sorry to admit are a touch overweight and a lot insecure. They are, however, the perfect complement to the M²s. They will take any abuse, obey any order, and still feel privileged that pretty people have given them the time of day. I am just like these women. Pathetically, I just think I am better than they are.

My entire life has revolved around women. They have been my friends, my decoys, my coworkers, my saviors, my nightmares. From birth, I have been women's sidekick, Tim Conway to their collective Carol Burnett. Even in my college fraternity, I was appointed "Sweetheart Chairman" because I knew how to handle women, make them laugh, manipulate the ladies to do what I wanted through listening and sensitivity. But that's getting harder and harder to do.

I sit for nearly two hours at our staff meeting, listening to these women drone on and on about the minutiae of their jobs. The dull conversation stands in stark contrast to the lush locales where we meet: ornate conference rooms that run the gamut from 1950s replicas of White House staterooms, to brand new, state-of-the-art conference rooms, where wood meets Warhol-decked walls, where wide windows overlook athletic fields, where laptops are hidden in mahogany tables, and screens and microphones pop up magically, unexpectedly, like spring crocuses.

I know that this is the one chance a week our secretaries and database entry clerks get to talk, to feel vital and important. And they do talk, on topics that range from the fluctuating office temperature to the latest Post-its to whose responsibility it is to clean the refrigerator. Lower back pain and the myriad of problems with our new phone system are topics that run closely behind.

Right now, they are talking about whose responsibility it is to change the toner in the copier.

I feel like my life is simultaneously stopped and slipping away in our staff meetings. I feel like, sitting here, my entire life is being wasted, that I am a fraud of the highest magnitude, that I bury my ambition and talent just for the safety that this comfortable conference chair provides.

Someone somewhere says that I never change the toner, and I remind them that I did it last time and that— *"Remember?"*—it exploded on my face, making me look like Al Jolson. No one seems to remember.

I roll my eyes, forgetting for a second that I'm not alone in my office. There is not an ounce of creativity in the room, not even a crackle of energy. In fact, our staff meetings induce comas. I look over at one of our heavyset, older secretaries, who looks exactly like Aunt Bee, without the apron or the warm personality; she is sound asleep. Snoring. She wakes suddenly and says she always changes the toner, someone else should do it. *How can she be sound asleep and still cognizant?* I roll my eyes again.

I think of my friend Cookie Henderson. Right now, I know she is probably doing the same thing at a similar staff meeting. I can imagine her here, looking over at me and rolling her eyes, too. I love Cookie. She has raised more money than Live Aid. She has told me that she estimates that she has raised over $100 million on her own. Her work is responsible for nearly every new building, classroom, computer, smart board, copper cupola, teak bench, wood chime, tolling bell, and engraved plaque on her campus. And there are a lot of those. Her campus tops ours in terms of grandeur. Cookie wears fitted, understated suits—herringbones and glen plaids—with silk blouses, her jackets decorated with elaborate spider pins and flowery brooches. Her silver hair is wavily stylish. Cookie is blind as a bat, and sports as many eyeglasses as she does pins. In fact, she changes her eyeglasses like she does her moods: Some days, she is vibrant, other days intellectual, some days saucy, and some coquettish. She always looks like a LensCrafters ad in an AARP magazine. Cookie is a huge sports fan, and she can play tennis like an aged Chris Evert, hitting the ball with the best alumni players, men or women. She does not like to lose, ever. She is battle-scarred and life-scarred. She has lost loved ones at too early an age, just like me.

Cookie is one of the only people professionally who knows I'm gay. She confessed this late one night after we had met for a drink after working an evening event.

"I've been through too much to care who you sleep with," she had said suddenly. "But a lot of people in this world we choose to work in would. They would chew you up and gulp you down if they knew, like a pack of bored, hungry lions. You be careful, my dear."

To this day, Cookie protects me like I am her blood.

A coworker nudges me out of my stupor, helping me out. "The invitations for the Alumni Dinner are at the printer, right, Wade? Doty needs to know right now."

"Yes, yes, they are," I reply, giving her a "Thanks for saving my ass again!" nod.

The conversation turns back to whose responsibility it is to order new office calendars.

I fade away again. To pass the time, I have invented a new game, one to replace my previous fun one of jabbing a pen as hard as I can into my thigh under the table. As soon as everyone is seated, I note the time and then wait to see how long it takes until one of the women finally cracks and goes to get a fresh Krispy Kreme doughnut or slice of Entenmann's coffee cake sitting in the boxes on the credenza in the conference room. I call this our "Dysfunctional Dessert Table." That's the name one of my friends has given his family's holiday dessert table, when his relatives stack roughly fifty desserts—cakes, pies, cupcakes, cookies, ambrosias—for approximately twenty people. As he explains it, "We all just take a sliver of every single one—a new dessert replacing the old one as soon as it's nicked—and eat out of nervousness or loneliness or embarrassment—whatever fuels us—until we are all human ticks."

The longest time the women in our office have gone without touching the Dysfunctional Dessert Table has been nearly twenty-three minutes, but that record came after most of us had just come from a breakfast meeting with our Alumni Association.

Already, I can feel the tension, could cut it with the knife that sits just a few feet away on top of an untouched bear claw. It is a barely controlled frenzy now, like in those movies where fishing boat captains throw raw meat into the blue ocean and wait for the sharks to circle. The women can barely listen to the staff reports; they nervously take fake notes, their eyes darting back and forth from the speaker to the doughnuts to their notepad to the strudel. After a few minutes, they begin to shift uncomfortably in their chairs, begin to chew the ends of their pens as though the hard plastic might somehow taste like sugary, fried dough. It doesn't.

Today, it takes only twelve minutes, just long enough for everyone to get seated and walked through the office supply updates, before someone breaks. She is already sweating a little in anticipation, and when she stands, I notice tiny sweat rings forming in the armpits of her ruffled polyester blouse, the kind that looks like she might have stolen it directly off the back of a circus clown. In her navy blue polyester pants and navy flats with damp orthotics, her thighs and shoes both make a "squish, squish, squish" sound as she heads for the table.

It's like falling dominoes now, everyone pushing their chairs out, a line forming at the boxes.

I used to be part of this routine. Food as comfort. It's the same for these women, who occasionally get abused by women who are thinner, prettier, and richer. I watch them work; our staff tries so hard to be nice, warm, customer friendly, but that emotion is too rarely reciprocated, except for an occasional box of chocolates or box of doughnuts that is sent after another spectacular event is finished.

Every woman takes only a single doughnut or pastry or slice of coffee cake at first, and then one encourages another to go get another, which they split, this rotation continuing until the boxes are empty and we break for lunch.

My Mornings with Miggie

Some Wednesday mornings I "babysit" Miggie.

Miggie Van Oxenhandler is an alumna who graduated, I think, in the late 1800s. Miggie was a socialite of great notoriety and she traveled the world. In her old age, and with nowhere else to go and nothing else to do, Miggie spent a couple of decades holed up in her library at home writing a never-quite-completed history of Tate, age and frustration occasionally eroding her once pristine language and delicate demeanor into that of a trucker. Now, she yells at anyone who knocks on her front door and mistakenly asks, "Can I come in?" with the phrase, "You mean, *May* I enter?!" To say the least, Miggie rarely has visitors. Save for me. I was only semijokingly asked during my original interviews to check in occasionally on Miggie, along with a few other wealthy women, to be their link to the school. However, my pop-ins now feel like an obligation.

Miggie always smells like a mix of Chanel No. 5, formaldehyde, and rubbing alcohol. She looks like a proud Nantucket grandmother, with her wicker handbags and nautical scarves tied around her neck. Her library, in fact, looks a lot like a lesbian's cottage in Nantucket: couches of ancient plaids, sailboat throw pillows, hand-carved rockers, handkerchief-covered lamps that throw off a dim glow and, lining the walls, hundreds of old photos of stern-looking alumnae or family members.

My routine is this: I usually arrive and enter Miggie's lair around 9:00 A.M. and check to see if she is awake and/or alive.

Miggie is always surly, in that grumpy next-door-neighbor sort of way.

"Miggie, good morning, sweetie. How are you today? *May* I enter?"

She is sleeping sitting up in her library, her silver hair perfectly coifed into a bun with an antique clip, a navy blue scarf with sailing knots tied around her neck, gray herringbone slacks and matching jacket over a sky blue silk blouse. She looks like an automated robot in a history museum featuring an exhibit on old, rich people.

I approach her quietly, kind of side-stepping my way up to her carefully, like you do an angry dog. I whisper again, "Good morning, sweetie. How are you today?"

"I'm just fan-fucking-tabulous. Why don't you scream a little louder next time? And there is never a need to say 'today,' unless you've time-warped from the past."

Miggie sounds like a Kennedy—same accent, same moneyed tone—albeit an angrier, coarser Kennedy. Yet, despite her tone, I'm always thankful the old bitch is alive. I wouldn't want the personal dilemma of deciding whether or not to actually call 911 or just leave her here propped up, door open, for someone to find. I have a nagging feeling I might do what the Mean Mommies would probably do: not call, since it would screw up their day. I imagine the Pink Ice Barbies would just drag her to the curb with a Magic Marker–inscribed postcard around her neck that said, "Old, dead alumna for pick-up."

"Glad to hear it," I say to Miggie. "Let me make you some fresh coffee. I brought some."

"*May* I make you some fresh coffee. *May* I. Oh, yum. Folgers. I'm thrilled Tate is kind enough to spring for the good stuff, considering I am leaving it half my estate. Can you puh-lease go to Starbucks and bring me a mocha? Pleeeasssee!"

This is a trap. I was told thirdhand she tricked someone before, and while they were gone, she took a cab to school and wandered the empty halls, screaming at the little girls in their "short skirts and catalog shoes." Despite this rumor, no one ever acts like there is really any problem, and so I simply watch her and help keep her busy in order to keep her happy, to keep her safe, to protect the fact that Miggie *supposedly* has Tate in her will for a lot of money.

"I can't leave," I say as usual to Miggie. "I have a meeting I need to get ready for." Which is true, if you can call xeroxing for M^2s a meeting.

"Never end a sentence with a preposition," she says, quickly followed by, "Do you like me?"

Miggie is needy today.

"I adore you!" I lie. "I never knew my grandmothers, and—I hope this isn't out of line to say—but you are the type of woman I always pictured them to be: strong-willed, smart, talented, independent, funny, and, of course, beautiful."

Her face lights up, and I can see, through the cracks and red veins and too much eye makeup, the face of the woman I have just described.

"You're full of it," she says, winking at me, "but it's a helluva good story. Where's my Folgers?"

I hand her a Tate coffee mug, complete with our historic crest, and she oh-so-slowly—her hand shaking the entire way—brings it to her mouth.

"Let me microwave you a muffin, OK?"

I stop.

"*May* I microwave you a muffin?"

She smiles, very pleased, and nods.

A mini-fridge in her library stays stocked with food, water, and soda to keep Miggie alert. I worry she only eats when I'm around. Her "assistant" is always on her cell phone. I have no idea how Miggie pulls herself together every morning. Willpower, I guess. Just like me.

"When do you leave for the Hamptons again?" I ask.

"Are you aiming for an invitation, young man?" she says. "I might just take you up on that."

"I'm more of a Midwest boy, I think."

"I think you're more of a . . . ," she says, trailing off. She looks at me and smiles, not bothering to finish.

"You can say whatever you're thinking," I say. "I can take it."

"I know you can, young man. You just don't need to take it. We've both taken our share of hits in our lives, haven't we?"

"I'll drink to that!" I say, clinking her coffee mug with mine.

And then I listen to Miggie reminisce for a while about the former headmaster, a handsome silver-haired man who could recite sonnets and speak Latin and send little shivers of desire down the spines of little, old alumnae; he led Tate for nearly forty years and will always be the greatest man ever to serve the school.

After staying for over an hour, I typically speed back to campus, avoiding the suburban cops, and sprint to the copy room to help the Pink Ice Barbies xerox flyers for a parent mailing. This task always proves incomprehensibly difficult for them, like trying to defuse a nuclear bomb. I endure paper cuts and paper jams and ink explosions while I watch them blow on their nails and apply lipstick, and listen to them gossip and rip their friends apart, like lions on a slow antelope, eyeing me up and down like I'm a deadly virus that has been leaked in through the air vents. Occasionally they will whisper things about me, as I squeeze by to pop in a thousand more sheets of pink paper, but I just ignore their looks, their whispers, considering most of their time is thankfully spent attacking fellow mothers and their "hideous handbags," or "bad blowouts," or "pale daughters."

While Miggie may sometimes be the biggest bitch in town, right now, she's one of the kindest women I know.

My Cup's Runneth Over

Every single one of my Thursdays is consumed with administrative meetings, which give me the same feeling as sitting around chugging Nyquil and watching C-Span on a cloudy day. Considering my little dilemmas pale greatly in comparison to more important topics, like raising money, disgruntled parents, or departing faculty, I say little. I always keep my problems to myself. Yet I always seem to walk out with about a month's worth of someone else's work.

This is why after these meetings I like to hide in the men's room until our administrators have a chance to scatter. This gives me a chance to walk alone across campus back to my office, enjoying the silence for a few moments, the kids playing, the few moments when I am not being chased or called by Kitsy.

This chilly early November fall morning, as I cross campus and pass by the Lower School playground, I notice a little boy standing alone along the fence, sticking bright red plastic cups into the chain link.

At first, I think the little boy is helping to spell out a "fence message." On special occasions, a different Lower School class will write a "fence message" using these plastic cups. The ends of the brightly colored cups are placed into the fence holes to spell out "Happy Valentine's Day!" or "Field Day—April 21!" or "Hey, Hey, It's May Day!" The messages—usually about three feet tall—are visible to parents in carpool as well as to cars that pass along the road by campus. They serve as Tate's kid-friendly, Nickelodeon-inspired billboards.

However, as I get closer, I see that the little boy has instead written "I'm Sad!" in red cups. Typically, Lower School students are never alone. They are surrounded by other kids, or teachers, or teachers' assistants, or mothers who stop to see their kids in the midst of their morning jogs or while walking their yellow Labs.

Hesitantly, I walk up to the little boy, who I now remember as being typically gregarious when I walk around campus snapping pictures.

"Hey. What're you doing?" I ask.

"Nothin'."

"What are you writing?"

"Nothin'."

"Why are you sad?"

"I don't know."

"You know, when you're sad, you need to tell someone. Do you want me to get your teacher?"

The little boy is thumping the ends of the cups nervously with his hands, like he is playing the bongos. He stops and looks up at me, his dark eyes filling with tears. His teeth are chattering in the wind, and I stick my fingers through the fence openings and zip his coat all the way up.

I look around nervously, hoping no one will see. I am constantly panicked that a moment like this will occur, that I will reach out to help and then be reported for being a pedophile. Don't laugh; I think it's the truth. If you're not the child's parent or a teacher who's beloved by the child's parent, I believe it's simply better to stay out of a situation.

And yet, I look into the little boy's eyes, which are silently begging me to listen. I can't walk away from him.

"Can you tell me why you're sad? I'd like to help."

And with that, the boy starts blubbering, shaking, his eyes growing stormy to match the gray morning.

"There's a birthday party this Friday, and everyone in our class got invited but me and another girl. How come everyone gets to go but us? It's not fair!"

I immediately feel like I've been punched in the stomach. The Lower School's policy is that every child is to be included in a student birthday party, if it falls during the course of a normal school year. The goal is to build friendships, to be inclusive, to treat everyone equally. It is a wonderful principle. It's a concept that I completely and totally support. School should always be about doing what's in the best interest of the child—*always*—not what's in the best interest of the parent.

Yet I know why this little boy wasn't invited—because I was never invited—why he might spend his whole school life here missing such parties. I can't tell the little boy why, though.

But I don't have to; he knows already. Even little kids know, and that's what hurts so much.

"It's because we're different, isn't it? We're not like the other families."

I feel like puking, and actually bend over and turn away from the little boy to hide my own tears.

"Are *you* OK?" he asks.

"I'm sad, too," I say, turning back around to look at the little boy.

And then I take a risk that I have been afraid to take during my tenure at Tate. "How about we try and make each other happy?"

And with that I circle around the fence and begin plucking out the red cups and tossing them into a nearby garbage container.

The little boy watches me for a minute and breaks into a big smile, before joining me in pulling his "I'm Sad" red cups.

"Deal!"

I don't realize that an M^2 is watching from the carpool lane, a mommy who has seen me and Gary together numerous times in town, once at an arts fund-raiser. She is a very Mean Mommy. I have seen her in the carpool and coffee klatches with Kitsy and the Pink Ice Barbies. Her name is Chachi. I remember this when I was introduced to her at the fund-raiser—before I could hide from her in the men's room—I smiled, and she didn't. She just stared at me, as though she'd like to smash a ceramic vase that was for sale over my head and then suck my brain out.

Chachi will report my interaction, couching it as a "curious interaction," I will later be told anonymously. I am instructed to always get a teacher first, that I should never intervene.

A little boy is struggling and hurt, and I'm not supposed to help? You are supposed to report it to his homeroom teacher.

Just like the little boy, I already know the real reasons why, and that's what really hurts so much.

Fluent Kitsy

Before Kitsy, my Fridays generally included taking photos at a never-ending smorgasbord of special events, like "Doughnuts & Dads," "Grandparents' Day," or "Spirit Day." Now, my Fridays typically center around Kitsy—planning for the weekend or the upcoming week.

This is why I'm not surprised to hear *"Hola, Señor Mantequilla!"* bellowing from my open door in early November. I turn and smile with the same enthusiasm as if Shakira had popped in to sing just for me.

Kitsy is learning Spanish. Every few weeks, it seems, she is learning a new language—Spanish, French, German, Dutch—walking around with tiny headphones clamped over her stiff blond bob, listening to Berlitz tapes and saying aloud, *"Donde esta el baño?"* She learns just enough, I know, to torture foreign hotel staff and concierge and waiters, angry they do not understand her broken phrases before asking, *"Esta stupido?"*

For some reason, she has been calling me *"Señor Mantequilla"* for weeks—"Mr. Butter" in English. She laughs every time she says it, kind of the way Joan Collins laughed mockingly at Linda Evans on *Dynasty*. This infuriates me. I don't really understand what's so funny, but I laugh, too, because I really do know Spanish, took four years of it in college, and, in my head, I'm saying, "*¡Cállate! ¡Puta estúpida!* (or "Shut up, you stupid bitch!"). That's the only dirty phrase I retained.

Still, that line really makes me laugh. Especially since I know she will be leaving right before our big Fall Dinner and torturing me long distance. How can Kitsy do something nice one minute and something so heinous the next? Why are the two always so inextricably linked?

Tate is nearing its four-day faculty-report-writing holiday break—it has sneaked up on me—and I suddenly have the sinking realization that my break will be spent doing Kitsy's work for the Fall Dinner. Especially after I tentatively ask her where she is going over break.

"Spain," she groans. "Of course, my husband would have to go *there* for business, not Greece, or the South of France. It gives me a chance to learn another language, though. That'll make, I think, six in which I'll be fluent, *Señor Mantequilla.*"

She laughs again. She doesn't ask me where I'm going because she doesn't care.

What she does care about is getting a record attendance for our Dinner, which is why she asks me to lunch.

In broken Spanish.

I officially say *"adios"* to my Friday.

I'd Like the $250,000 Cobb Salad, Please

Kitsy takes me to lunch at her Country Club, which happens to be one of the oldest, most influential private clubs in town. To become a member, I've heard, you must be recommended by three current members, pass an infinite series of interviews with the city's VIPs, upper crust and societal leaders, have your family's genealogy tracked, studied, and verified, and then, ultimately, be able to pay the annual high-six-figure club fee. That last part of the equation can prove to be the trickiest for a lot of families, even the most wealthy and connected, since there's no convenient payment plan available. You either have the cash, or you don't.

In advance of our Fall Dinner—our major, annual event for hundreds—Kitsy wants me to see "true elegance," witness firsthand how servers should "behave," taste how great food should be "presented and prepared." She wants to be assured that I, in advance of her departure, understand how the event should be run. She doesn't care that this is an annual event, and, though stressful, a well-oiled routine. She only cares that this event become *her* event, that it exceed any of our expectations, demolish any past attendance record.

When we are seated, she quickly quizzes me on what I have learned so far in her Wealthy Woman 101 etiquette class today.

"What is the only thing my Club does incorrectly, etiquette-wise?" she asks me.

Discriminates? I think.

"You should know this," she says, in an exasperated tone.

I have taken a bite of a sesame seed breadstick and can feel the seeds sticking between my teeth. I know if I speak, or smile, or open my mouth right now I will look like my teeth are rotten. I will look like a hillbilly without dental insurance.

"Cat got your tongue?" she asks.

I shrug my shoulders.

"Oh, Wade," she says disappointedly, her blue eyes looking just like the gas pilot light in our cabin's old stove on Sugar Creek. "Valet service is five dollars per car. That is just tacky. Do you know what we pay to be members here? Valet service should be free. Coat check should be free. And we should not be expected to tip on top of that, to pull dollar bills from our pockets like we're at a Laundromat. I'm quite certain the service staff is well compensated. A dollar here and a dollar there is just gauche. I refuse to tip now—all my friends refuse to tip now—just out of protest. Now you know."

I smile, tight-lipped, and nod. I pretend to study the menu, trying to work the seeds out of my teeth.

My God! A house salad is twenty-seven dollars. A hamburger is thirty-two dollars. A seed dislodges and sticks in my throat. I choke and take a big drink of water, which I aspirate. Kitsy is staring at me, aghast, like a circus freak has been seated with her and is eating nachos with cloven hooves. I excuse myself to the men's room, where I scream after being startled by a black attendant standing ready with a hot, white hand towel.

"What are you doing in here?" I ask.

"I work here, sir," he says.

"In a bathroom?" I ask.

"Yes, sir. Do you need a hand towel?"

"Not really. But do you have any floss?"

He does. Of course.

"Thanks," I say, looking at his nametag. "Sam."

I return to the table and begin to take my seat, when Kitsy yanks a dryer sheet off my back. "Do you need this?" she asks loudly, laughing at her joke, waving my friend Bounce around like a warning flag. "Girls, girls, I surrender!"

I look over. The Pink Ice Barbies have just been seated and have been watching this little interaction—riveted and amused—like Kitsy is lunching with the Elephant Man.

"Oh, my God!" she now whispers conspiratorially, after publicly humiliating me. "Didn't you know it was there?"

I didn't know. I was in a hurry this morning. I am not perfect.

All I really do know is that I am eating in a Country Club that I don't think would ever have me as a member. It has been a topic of local conversation for years because of its lack of "inclusiveness" and "equity." There have been rumored lawsuits for years.

Our server arrives with my food. While I was in the bathroom, Kitsy ordered for me. And, I have to admit, she has great taste and understands my taste, no matter how undeveloped it might be.

I start with a glass of imported water, which I sip while sitting on a terrace filled with tropical flowers and plants and servers who don't make a sound as they walk. I sit on a terrace surrounded by every mover and shaker in town.

And this makes me feel very fulfilled, very happy with myself, despite the feeling that at any moment I might simply be pulled from my white-clothed chair and beaten senseless behind the club's dumpsters by tattooed men whose bodies look like refrigerators. Right now, however, this seems like a fair price to pay in order to take in the absolute grandeur of this place: the grounds, the decor, the white tuxed servers, the old wood, the hushed quiet of a place that only old money can cushion.

So I laugh at Kitsy's jokes and listen to her boss around the wait staff and pass notes written in pink lipstick on Country Club napkins to the Pink Ice Barbies, like we're all still in fifth-grade homeroom. I do this because I get to eat the salmon, which is the chef's special. And the Country Club cobbler with a cappucino. I have never been in a Country Club, much less one this storied, this incredible. And, now that I've been here, I'd like to be invited back.

Until Kitsy stiffs our waiter on a $150 tab. "Silent protest," she says to me, in front of him, signing her member's bill with a pink lipstick immediately after retouching her perfect, pouty lips.

"Excuse me for a just a moment," I say, heading for the bath-room, ignoring her horrified reaction.

I open the men's room door and yank two ten-dollar bills—it's all I have—from my wallet. "Sam, I forgot to give you this earlier. I'm sorry. And could you give one to our waiter when you see him? Just ask; he'll remember us."

Sam stares at me like I am covered in dryer sheets. "Thank you, sir," he says, a bit cautiously.

"No problem. At least I get vision and dental to put up with all this crap."

Sam stares at me again, and holds out a hot, white hand towel. Standing like this, he looks exactly like the lawn ornament of the black jockey some locals have in their yards. I thought they had banned these statues in the 1960s.

"Nothin's really changed," I hear the black grandmother saying in my head. "Nothin's changed."

I take the hand towel and wipe down my face.

"I thought you could use that," Sam says.

The Not-So-Silent Auction

The goal of Tate's big Fall Dinner is to honor alumni who have already been honored numerous times in their lives and also to raise money for Tate. All necessary and noble goals.

Kitsy has been in Spain for the past two weeks—she extended her stay in Costa del Sol to "recharge her batteries and get a real tan"—but has returned just in time for the event. In a suite reserved for her personal use, I try to provide her with a brief summary of everything that has transpired over the last two weeks—buying medals for the honorees, creating a five hundred-picture archival PowerPoint presentation, directing a ten-minute tribute video for the honorees, reshaping centerpieces, purchasing gifts for presenters— as well as try to run through the order of the evening. Very little sticks. She is too concerned about her appearance to worry about such trivial matters. If everything is a disaster, I will be beheaded. If everything is a success, I will be ignored. For some reason, standing in the suite watching Kitsy primp, I imagine her as a self-obsessed, ADD passenger tasked with radioing for emergency help on the *Hindenburg.* "There seems to be a little puh-roblem on this nasty little balloon. TTFN!"

She waves me away with a lipstick as she reapplies for the tenth time tonight. "I need to run through my remarks now. TTFN!" She waves a perfectly manicured hand bye-bye at me, like she's trying to make me disappear. And I do.

Kitsy has personally annointed herself as a presenter for tonight's event. We had wanted to secure famous alumni, but the M²s must have their moment in the sun.

I secretly pray, considering she's been gone so long, that she will stumble in her heels, or mispronounce a name. But she doesn't, because I reminded her to scrape the bottoms of her new heels with sandpaper and we have phonetically spelled out every awkward word or name, just like at Commencement. I miss no detail, and she doesn't miss a beat. Never mind that she is Hollywood tan and looks fabulous in a long, pink, embroidered, fitted jacket and shimmery pants that hug her legs like a second skin.

The dinner goes perfectly, although I only have time to chug three glasses of wine and eat the top off a hardened dinner roll, pulling these items off quickly moving trays from behind the stage as the wait staff brings back diners' leftovers. I look out into the crowd from my heightened perch. For once, I have the best perspective, one that is higher than everyone else's. Doty is sitting near the front, with some of the night's honorees, wearing what I think is a toga. Everyone is ignoring him. Cookie is in attendance, seated at a table with some high rollers, old men who are all eighty-plus and friends of some of our honorees. She is laughing lamely at the joke of a man whose bald head is covered with age spots, and pretending as though his hand is not on her thigh. Our staff is seated at a table that is so far in the back of the ballroom that it is not even lit, almost out the back doors. Half of the staff are asleep. I watch the PowerPoint presentation, trying to make sense of the pictures that are flashing—from my perspective—backward on a big screen in front of me. I get dizzy and drink more wine.

At the end of the night, Kitsy departs without even thanking me for my efforts.

I hate her.

That is until she sends me front row seats and VIP parking for *Miss Saigon* the next morning along with a fifty-dollar gift card to Starbucks.

Wade Gets Organized

I am thumbing through a Boise office supply catalog, marking the items I need to make myself a highly functioning, highly organized mover and shaker.

Infinite number of rainbow-colored binders and folders? Check. Coordinating highlighters? Check.

Intricate Post-it project tracking system? Check.

It seems my life is a shambles. That's what I am told anyway by Doty and the organizational coach he has hired to "change my life." My coach's name is Delphinium. Like the flower. Delphinium, however, is not pretty and delicate like her namesake. The Latin translation must mean "thorny bitch."

Her work basically boils down to white-collar closet organization. The organizational piece de resistance I receive is a "My-Time Desk Planner," which I am told will "help me effectively achieve my goals."

"It takes time to save time," Delphinium tells me. I have no idea what this means, but she presents me with a thick, chocolate brown, leather calendar. It looks how I imagine Donald Trump's wallet to be—overstuffed, new and shiny, yet never to be used in everyday life.

I open the first page of my calendar, which lists a set of directions called "The Ten Commitments." It seems that it will take me anywhere between five and eight hours a month *just to organize my calendar.* Delphinium tells me I must start each day by planning and prioritizing, use my notes page to record all my commitments and promises for the day, chart my daily progress toward unfinished goals, and, most importantly, carry my calendar with me at all times. "Your calendar is your life. It is your new accessory. Just think of it as your watch."

My new watch already weighs five pounds, and it is not complimentary to my overall look at all. Rather, from a distance, I look like I have a leather cyst on my thigh.

My My-Time calendar breaks my days into microscopic increments, as though it is possible for me to accomplish hundreds of two-minute tasks every single day. The calendar has bare spots for "Action Steps," "Imperatives," "Today's Accomplishments," and "Contacts" and "Follow-Ups." On the back of each day is a blank page entitled "Affirmations." I didn't realize I was an unorganized alcoholic. My favorite part of my My-Time calendar is the ever-present "Wheel of Life," a page that appears throughout the calendar, like God's eye. The Wheel of Life looks like a giant roulette wheel with the word "You" as its bulls-eye. Surrounding the wheel are categories like "Career and Work," "Mental and Educational," "Family and Home," "Spiritual and Ethical," "Social and Cultural," "Financial and Security," and "Physical and Health."

"Your Wheel of Life is constantly in motion," Delphinium tells me, "and it's up to you to stop it at the right place at the right time each day."

"Why doesn't my Wheel of Life have 'Carpool,' or 'Go to the Grocery Store,' or 'Throw Away Dog Poop in the Backyard'?"

Delphinium doesn't laugh. I don't know if she's even capable of a chuckle.

I try again. I feel compelled to break her.

"So my Wheel of Life is kind of like a Zen Las Vegas thing, right?"

More silence.

"Have you ever been visited by your Wheel of Life in a dream?"

Nothing. I give up.

In addition to my pretty calendar, I also end up with new file cabinets and hanging, color-coded files, and project folders on my Mac desktop. My piles of paper and project "stacks" are hidden from public view, and my beloved manic ideas, which I constantly scratch on Post-its and slap around my office, are simply tossed. When Delphinium is finished, my office looks like the isolation room at a sanitarium. I suddenly feel naked and very, very unproductive.

I know I cannot work in this environment. I will go nuts. I will spend my days organizing, or trying to stay organized, rather than being creative.

Organization is very big at Tate. More importantly, the image of organization is important. We must look like winners. Winners use binders and color-coordinated folders, they don't stack and pile like the Unabomber. That's just odd. This school doesn't like odd.

I am asked in a subsequent performance review about my lack of organization.

"Don't kids learn differently? Don't people work differently? Aren't people different?" I ask, perhaps a bit indignantly, realizing too late that I sound exactly like the dummy in "Magic." "Aren't our differences what makes Tate tick, the world tick, what makes it such an interesting place?"

"Are you seeking attention?" I am asked in return.

"I'm just being myself," I answer.

"That seems to be a problem," they answer.

I Get an "E" for "Effort"

I am hiding under Doty's desk.

It is 6:00 P.M., already dark in mid-November, and everyone has left the office. I stayed to pretend-work late. I really just wanted to sneak into Doty's office so I could search through his file cabinet and see what he has written about me in his review.

I am semihunched, staying low to the ground, so no one will see my shadowy figure, using the penlight on one of our Tate keychains to navigate. I steal into his office and begin snooping. I rifle through his desk. Everything is organized in a rainbow of color-coded files, which are stacked and Post-it'ed and marked and deadlined and initialed in more colors; it looks like a bag of Skittles has exploded. I glimpse at his desktop calendar, which is scritched and scratched, filled with meetings followed by exclamation points. And then I see it:

Saturday: Leaf Management!

Sunday: Spiritual Review!

It finally hits me: I work for a whacko who assigns corporate buzzwords to raking and church.

Undeterred, I remain crouched and hunker over to the giant cherry filing cabinet that sits by Doty's window overlooking our manicured campus.

The cabinet is locked. I hunker back over to Doty's desk and grab a jumbo-sized paperclip. I knee-walk back over to the cabinet, partially unwind the paperclip and jiggle it around, over, and under the lock. I hear a click. My God, it actually worked. Watching *Mac-Gyver* for so many years has finally paid off.

I randomly open a drawer. It's the "R" drawer. Perfect. It should be under "R" for Rouse, or Review, right? No.

"W" for Wade? No.

"S" for Staff. No.

"H" for HR? No.

How the hell does he organize this?

So I start from the beginning of the alphabet, my only option. Twenty minutes later, I am still flicking through his zillion color-coded, alphabetical files, knowing he will never look at any of these again in his life. It just looks good. It's just what he thinks he has to do. Manage his time. Manage others. Never actually accomplish anything on his own. Doty's assistant does all this, and he has gone through numerous assistants over the years. One, ironically enough I was told, was color-blind, the single fact that was not discerned through the three-week interview process. In Doty's colorfully organized world, being color-blind is a primo defect.

My review, of course, is under "F" for "Fiscal Year" instead of "Finally, I found the fucking thing." *Your system makes perfect sense, Doty.*

I begin thumbing through my review, reading it with my penlight. It says, more or less:

"Wade is smart and creative but not organized and efficient. He needs to improve his time-management skills. He needs to focus on the work, not the people. He is too sensitive. He is too easily influenced by others."

Jesus. Is he a manager or a new-age psychologist?

My review also implies that I am a passable writer, but that I need to hone my speech-writing skills. (See Diversity Presentation.) I am close to committing hari-kari with my penlight when I hear our main office door squeak open. I panic, my heart racing. I close the file drawer and look around desperately in the dark, like Lucy Ricardo.

Doty's light goes on. I am scrunched in a ball on my hands and knees under his desk, his office chair pulled tightly against my face. At first, I think it is the night janitor, picking up the trash. But then I smell Old Spice. *Doty!*

He is looking on his desk for something, shuffling papers, scouring through his in- and out-boxes. I can hear him breathing. I can hear him humming something. Something I hate. "You Raise Me Up" by Josh Groban.

Part of me wants to jump up and scare the shit out of him, to bash him over the head with his own phone a few times and scamper into the darkness.

But, for once, my skill at saying nothing pays off. I hold my breath, my body still. Doty grabs something and hums his skin-colored, Sansabelt-slack-wearing ass back out of the office.

I stay hunkered down, still shaking, still scared, still horrified that I am sneaking into offices, stealing and disposing of confidential information, and hiding under desks on my hands and knees.

Who have I become? But I already know. *I have become Doty. I have become Kitsy. I have become the Pink Ice Barbies. I have become everything I thought I despised.*

But those thoughts are quickly replaced by one main thought: Thank God I told Doty to get the modesty panel when he ordered his new desk so he could "impose a wall of confidence and barrier of power" to his visitors.

Do You Guys Know
Sean Connery?

I feel like I've been kidnapped and forced to shoot a Scottish porn video.

For the last hour, I have hidden four bagpipers in Kitsy's basement, which is really a home theater the size of a six-screen movie multiplex. The bagpipers smell like wool, English leather, and whiskey. Every few minutes, they pull flasks from the waistbands of their kilts and drink something strong; I can't tell if it's cologne or liquor. I would be turned on a little bit by this whole scene if the bagpipers weren't pushing three hundred, in both years and pounds.

Tate has just defeated its rival in football, and Kitsy is having a post-party. Football is God at Tate. It is the sport of kings; it is the sport that can sometimes bring out the worst in the M^2s.

I was asked at the last minute by Kitsy to take photos of her party following the big game. I consider weekend events such as this to be personal in nature—they certainly ruin my weekends, add tension to my relationship with Gary—but Kitsy would not take no for an answer, saying it was vital that I capture these people and this moment for the archives of Tate, so people could look back on this moment forever.

Thing is, no one will ever want to reflect on this low point in our history. And no one will ever know I am here.

When I arrive in my Toyota Corolla, I see that Kitsy has nearly one hundred people on her patio, which sits fairly close to the football stadium of a football rival. The slate patio is only slightly smaller than a field itself. The crowd is chugging Bloody Marys and Heinekens, even some of the teenaged kids.

I realize too late that my invitation as the photographer is only a ruse. I am immediately captured by Kitsy upon my arrival like an errant butterfly. Kitsy, who has somehow managed to incorporate pink into her blue and gold fan's attire, escorts me down the back stairs into her home theater, where I am promptly greeted by a group of old, fat men wearing skirts. They start to blow on their bagpipes—some sort of bizarrely upbeat dirge blasting forth—before Kitsy starts screaming, "Shut up! Shut up!" When they quiet, Kitsy looks at me says, "Watch them, Wade. Not a sound until you hear from me." I am here to babysit the bagpipers, to keep them quiet, to be called on as the sober spokesperson for the group in case any school VIPs drop by unexpectedly.

I am couch-bound for an hour, staring at the crotches of the bagpipers, who sit with their legs spread apart, like Sharon Stone in *Basic Instinct. Didn't their mothers teach them to cross their legs while wearing a dress?* Finally, Kitsy appears, staggering just a little, sloshing tomato juice down her wrist. "Here," she says, waving a check in front of my face. I have never seen her like this; I am stunned and staring open-mouthed. *"Here!"* she slurs again. I take the check and look at it. It is for $4,000. These are some pricey pipers. I look again. It is made out simply to what could be "The Bagpipers" in a drunken scrawl. I wonder briefly if the check will clear with this in the "Pay to" line, but this is not my issue, so I simply hand it over to the oldest, fattest guy.

"Itsshh time," Kitsy slurs, and we head up the steps, where the crowd is loud and liquored. Kitsy gathers everyone on her lawn—

it is a spectacular late fall day, the trees a literal fireworks of color, the leaves barely clinging to the branches—and she motions for me to take photos. The group is caustic and demeaning. I am affectionately called "Ansel Adams," "Tate's lapdog," "Pretty boy" and even, once, "Cocksucker." They will not remember their words tomorrow.

Someone notices today, however.

"Are you OK?" Mitsy asks me.

"Yeah," I say unconvincingly to one of the few people here, besides me, who isn't drinking.

"You don't look OK," she says, before skipping away into the massive expanse of green.

Then Kitsy screams, "Ssshurprisshe! Hit it, boyssshh!" and the bagpipers start playing, a beloved tradition at Tate.

I try to hide in the home theater, locked in the dark, not wanting anyone else to know that I am here, just wanting to endure and make it out unscathed. Until I hear my name being bellowed as if through a bullhorn by Kitsy.

"WWWWWAAAAAAAADDDDDDDEEEE!!!!!"

Jesus. It *is* Kitsy. And she *is* yelling through a bullhorn.

I emerge from the shadows.

Kitsy is standing with a neighbor, an elderly gentleman who I know attended a rival institution. He is a patron of the city and a philanthropist to his alma mater. The distinguished man looks like Christopher Plummer. He is, to say the least, not pleased with anything about this afternoon: his school's lopsided defeat to its archrival, the behavior of this crowd, the spectacle that is Kitsy.

"Wade Rousshh ish our PR pershon. He can shpeak to you about ush."

Kitsy has called me to save her ass. I know what to do already, how to handle this situation. I am a pro at it. Without thinking, I go into mommy-handling mode. Kitsy doesn't even have to say another unintelligible word.

"Can I speak with you, sir?" I ask the man as politely as an English street urchin begging for a bread crumb. We walk into the yard. Kitsy is trying to listen to us. She is holding a Tate bullhorn up to her ear; she looks like the RCA dog. "Mrs. Ludington just learned last week that she had a miscarriage. She is not herself. Her friends thought they could cheer her with a little party today. It was an inappropriate idea on every level."

Christopher Plummer is studying me closely, like a jury foreman, trying to deduce if I am lying.

"You know of Mrs. Ludington and her connections in town?" I ask, a threat posed as a question. It is one of my favorite tactics in crisis situations like this. I let the question sit for a second. It has no impact. Christopher Plummer doesn't even shake his silvery gray head in agreement. His school's parents and alumni are as important and influential as ours. But they definitely aren't as rich. I go in for the kill. "Mrs. Ludington very seriously wants another child. And I strongly believe she would like that child to attend your school. She is not pleased with the leadership of our institution right now. Why do you think she purchased her residence so close to your campus? She is thinking of making the switch, of ending her long legacy with Tate. Can you imagine the uproar?"

Christopher Plummer is practically wetting himself, dreaming now of how he can announce this to friends and his school, how he can take credit for this coup. I can see him dreaming of standing next to Kitsy as she hands him a check in the range of $10 million. This will never happen.

"We'll let it go this time," he says suddenly, cheerily to me, like I've just simply cheated in croquet, jokingly nudged the ball through the wicket with my foot while he wasn't looking. "It's all in good fun, right? There's nothing like a heated rivalry!"

He marches away. Kitsy makes her way down to me shakily, in slow motion, stop-action, like one of those pathetic, drunken redneck women who get arrested on *Cops*. Her blue eyes are rimmed in red, but they are beaming.

"You're gooooood," she says. "Maybe even better than me."

This last sentence actually sounds like "Maypole efen buttering me."

Kitsy reaches out to tap me on the side of the head, like the football team does after a good play; in trying this tricky bit of coordination, she spills the illegal Bloody Mary she is holding, actually tossing it into the center of my Tate sweatshirt.

"Ohmygawd. I sho shorry. Thash jush a cheapol sweatyshirt anyhoo. It'll c'mout. Don'choo tell anyone about today, OK?"

I try to interpret what Kitsy has said. I can't. I look at her shimmying back to her friends—Chachi, the Pink Ice Barbies and their husbands—who are all applauding like monkeys. The majority of our parents are already back at home, or at a nearby restaurant, having a nice, quiet celebratory dinner with their families, embracing everything important and valued about a day like today. And yet, in one afternoon, the person who I thought was supposed to embody all that is good about Tate, embody all that is wonderful about the amazing benefits of private education—has pulled a Courtney Love.

I look down at my sweatshirt. It looks like I've been shot. I'm not mad. Actually, since I will never develop these photos, I'm thrilled there's at least some physical evidence of the crime that has been committed today.

Mitsy's a Mess

I have become obsessed with watching Mitsy. I know it's bizarre and a little disturbing, but I want to see the little girl that sprang from Kitsy's head, like Zeus. I need to believe that she will not be an exact replica of her mommy.

Really, I am worried about her. I worry that she is not OK. Like a lot of kids here at Tate. So I stand at her classroom door, or on the playground, or in the lunchroom pretending to take pictures.

On the surface, Mitsy is the perfect child, a miniature Kitsy. She is blond, pretty, pink and adorable, like Dakota Fanning. She is bright and charming, just like a child actor, saying all the right things, smiling at all the right times, asking all the cute questions, just like perfect kids do.

But when you see Mitsy out of class, out of the teachers' eyes, out of her mother's reach, out of the spotlight, she is a different child. Many of these kids become different children.

Mitsy cries when her shoelace is untied, or panics when her dress gets dirty on the playground. She hits other children, hard and with clear intention, when they refuse to do what she says in the hallway. At six, perfection, order, and control are already cornerstones of Mitsy's existence.

Sometimes the desire to reach out and shake her overwhelms me, because I know there is a wonderful, caring, sensitive little girl in there. I don't want that to disappear, not yet.

This afternoon, as I pass her on the playground, I stop. She is playing on a kid's sculpture of a turtle, one where children can climb up its tail and ride down its shell, like a slick slide. I stop and ask if I can take her picture for our alumni magazine. It is a windy late November day, and the two ponytails on each side of her head—tied with neon pink silk ribbons—are being blown from left to right, right to left, front to back, back to front, spinning in circles.

"Noooooooooooooo!" she screams, tears forming immediately in her eyes and quickly running down her reddened cheeks. "You can't! I'm ugly right now. And my mommy wouldn't want any ugly pictures of me! She hates ugly people!"

I lower my shaking camera and kneel in front of this little girl. "You're not ugly, Mitsy. You're beautiful. It's just windy, that's all. Not everyone can be perfect all the time, can they?"

She tilts her head, just like my dog Marge does, and thinks about this. Suddenly, without warning, she reaches up and undoes one of her pink ribbons, releasing it, letting it go in the wind, where it quickly takes flight, like a pink birthday balloon, as if she's just made the most important wish of her life. Her remaining ponytail whips in the wind, and she grabs and releases that ribbon, too, her hair now a carnival, flying, whirling, standing on end.

She is giggling, screaming, her hands over her head, feeling her hair flying freely, going wherever it wants, no one there to tame it for once.

"Are *you* OK?" I ask her.

She nods, laughing.

"How do you feel?" I ask, lifting the camera to my eye.

"Like a kid!" she giggles.

I snap the photo.

Leaf Me Alone

During a simple, five-minute walk through our halls, I hop, jump, skip, leap, or weave around the circular sides of an endless number of ornate, ancient, bronzed Tate Academy crests and seals that are embedded in the terrazzo and wood-herringbone floors. It is law here: No member of the Tate community is allowed to step on these seals; everyone must walk around them, swim around them like salmon avoiding mountain rocks. Even babies are scolded by their mothers for making contact. These crests are like the Pope's ring. A gentle, respectful kiss is the only appropriate contact.

I have worked at Tate long enough to know this, yet I still forget this, every single day, even though these crests and seals are shined and polished and sit shimmering in the middle of the floors—incapable of being ignored—like a UFO that hovers above the Nebraska farmlands.

Yet, I am always so preoccupied—running to carpool or a meeting, honing what I will say to Kitsy or another M^2, yoga chanting to center myself—that I always happen upon these crests, jumping at the last minute, like an equestrian's horse over a high fence. It looks like I'm getting electroshock therapy at the very last minute to help me remember this important piece of Tate etiquette. Kids gasp at my lack of respect, the fact that this is not yet engrained into my head even after years of working here.

It's just that everything here seems so damn perfect. So pretty. So staged. I cannot keep up with the image that is portrayed to the public; the problem is, I am supposed to be the defender of that image. I have a defective gene, many defective genes, I try hard to cover, like dirty laundry you shove under the bed when visitors unexpectedly pop by.

In spring, our campus looks better than our city's revered botanical garden. In summer, the magnificent, ancient trees arch their limbs to provide leafy, shaded canopies over every walkway and bench.

Even at the height of fall, when these trees are shedding their leaves as quickly as little kids do their coats when they hit the front door, there is still never a stray leaf on campus. Or an errant weed popping through the overflowing windowboxes, or a smear on any door or window, or even a lonely pencil eraser in the hall. When I am not being chased by the mommies, I spend my work days getting chased by leaf blowers and hoes and Windex and dust mops. At Tate, the quest for perfection begins at home, continues through the halls and classrooms, onto the stages and athletic fields, into sessions with tutors and piano teachers, and ends with homework.

This quest for perfection at Tate starts, literally, at birth.

By the age of two, the choice of nursery school becomes vitally important to the rich of our city, so babies are coached to smile and draw circles and play well with others, because at two they must be able to show these skills to selection committees at the top-tier nursery schools.

"Look at her share her bear," an admissions counselor might exclaim. "How exquisite!"

Even at two, the pressure is on babies to perform above expectation. But the pressure is also on these preschools to meet parental expectations. The glossy promotional admissions materials of these nursery schools, above all else, tout the day-school matriculation list—all wanting to list Tate as the number one destination—as well as the *college* destinations of their previous classes, the three- and four-year-olds who graduated a decade and a half ago. Of course, all logic aside, finger painting did help little Sally get into Cornell, right?

Life for these families is all about what's known in our city as "The List": private school, ACT scores, and the Ivies rule all. Children must make The List, they must prove their mettle, and belonging to some arbitrary list is the only way to stand above the crowd. No matter how hard Tate tries to emphasize life beyond the Dean's list and the college matriculation list and the National Merit list, it always comes back to a list of some sort, a quest to be named to something that is deemed to be the best by someone else.

Childhood for many wealthy kids in our city is spent preparing for admission to the Ivies. Questions constantly loom, forever damning the magical journey and exploration of youth: Do I play field hockey or water polo, how many AP courses do I need to take, what community service looks best, who do I know that's a legacy who can write a rec letter for me? For some, it no longer matters if a particular college is actually a good fit for the child, if the student will actually be happy there, so long as it meets the expectation of Tate and the parents. A Tate student's college destination completes "The List" for everyone: students, parents, alumni, trustees, Tate itself. I sit in endless meetings hearing parents talk about how my alma mater, Northwestern, is "an OK" last resort, behind thirty other schools.

On a fall walk back to my office following another meeting, I find myself being chased yet again by a man with a leaf blower, and realize that if every leaf can be controlled and contained, so can the spontaneity and wonder of life and of children. So can my life.

Every action can be controlled so it fits according to Tate's plan of perfection.

I return to my little office with its big windows and admire the mess that surrounds me. I have already given up color-coordinating and organizing by file folder; I still stack and pile by project. The desktop on my computer again looks like an unstarted puzzle. My mess makes me happy but it also makes me sad. I do everything well, but nothing right, it seems. I would not make a List here, I don't think.

I move a pile of press releases and call my mother, just because I need to hear her voice, knowing her rambling will distract me from this place. And it works.

She announces to me, as though she is telling me she has run out of paper towels, that my father, for a brief period of time an hour or so ago, had been on fire.

It seems that while he was burning leaves in a ditch at the big house, he had set himself ablaze—not bothering to bring the hose down with him while he burned—and had, indeed, been engulfed in flames for a few seconds before my mother walked to the front porch and screamed, "Ted! Drop and roll!"

Which he finally did, putting himself out.

"The old fart's fine. I just rubbed a stick of butter all over his burned body."

I am thankful, of course, that my father is not injured. I am just as thankful, however, that I grew up in a family that let me make mistakes, had the confidence to let me choose my own course.

I am thankful to have grown up knowing people who struggled for years to make it through community college, but for whom the experience was transformational and inspirational, more so than the many people I know here who skated through the Ivies.

Mostly, I am thankful I grew up in a family that simply lets the leaves pile up and occasionally sets itself on fire.

One No-Fat, No-Whip Loogy Latte, Please!

I have quickly developed an unspoken understanding with April, the chubby barista at a neighborhood coffeeshop. She will use whole milk in Kitsy's latte, and I will keep my mouth shut, my silence earning me a free grande white mocha each time I come in and April is working.

Like most good things, our understanding is forged on revenge. The very first time I meet Kitsy at this coffeeshop for a morning meeting—it's her new favorite place to meet outside of the carpool lane—she tells the young barista, casually, as though she's offering a compliment, "You know what's funny? I've never met a thin April."

Shocked, the chubby girl with dark hair and sad eyes, who looks like the daughter of Ann Wilson, the lead singer of Heart, drops the silver canister she is holding, hot milk exploding up and onto her legs.

"Maybe I should just call you 'Grace' instead," Kitsy says, laughing at April's klutziness. Then she turns to me and says, "Sit!" like she is commanding LulaBelle, and stalks her way to the ladies' room, a flash of jarring pink against the cool, calming, earthy colors of the coffee house.

When she disappears, April looks over at me, dripping and soaked, and holds up a gallon of whole milk. I say nothing; *technically,* I never really grant April my OK, but it is understood that my silence is a stamp of approval.

I initially feel bad about this, until Kitsy emerges from the bathroom and tells April to add a dash of cinnamon to the top of her no-fat, no-whip, sugar-free vanilla latte.

"No, April, no!" Kitsy screams at the girl when she starts shaking the spice canister. "The cinnamon is supposed to *dance* across the top, not *clot!* You'll do better next time, won't you? Can I speak with your supervisor?"

An hour later, my notebook is filled with suggestions and ideas on how to better the next event on Tate's calendar—Tate's beloved Holiday Concert in early December—and the head of April's supervisor is filled with ways to improve not only her performance but also the performance of this particular franchise. Satisfied with her brilliance for the morning, Kitsy stands to leave.

"I feel so full," she says. "I guess I shouldn't have had that Zone bar after my early-morning workout."

As we depart, I turn to look at April through the tinted window of the coffeehouse. She is smiling. It is the first time she has done so all morning.

In Her Shoes

When I want to hide from Kitsy, I retreat into a classroom. This not only allows me forty-five minutes of peace but also reminds me of why we are all here at Tate, of the incredible advantages these lucky children are getting. The faculty are miracle workers.

There is nothing more thrilling that watching a Lower School child make a connection, or earn confidence, or begin to read. I like to watch young children take a first stab at writing poetry, or finger painting their family; their creativity is limitless, most have not yet put up walls, their parents' words have not yet sunk in: *You will be a doctor, or a lawyer, or an engineer. You will focus on math and science, not English or music.* Right now, they can be little artists. They can be whatever they want.

Sometimes, I walk from Lower School, to Middle School and then Upper School, pretending to take photos for publications or for our Web site but really with the intention of seeing the evolution of children, both good and bad.

I see miracles happen in class, and then I see them destroyed as soon as the kids walk into the halls. I am not saying this happens every day to every child, but I see it too often to dismiss it.

In a single walk, covering campus and spanning just an hour one day, I witness the beauty and horror of youth.

On my way through the Lower School, I watch a teacher lead her class from the art room back to her homeroom. Her students have made pots, and on the trek through the cafeteria, a little boy trips and drops his, the tiny pot crashing into pieces. The boy begins crying, inconsolable, and the teacher stays to comfort him, sending the kids back to their room. When she returns with the upset boy in tow, the class surprises them by presenting their "new" pots, which they have purposely broken and then quickly glued back together.

"We wanted our pots to have character," says a little girl. I quickly learn that the first-graders have been studying the concept of "character" by reading fairy tales. "And we didn't want him to feel bad."

It is one of the most touching things I have ever witnessed.

Still, later that same morning, as I make my way through the hallway, the Barbies have a classmate secretly cornered in the hall— a cute little girl who gets dropped off in a rusting Ford pickup an hour before the other kids even start to arrive. The Barbies say this to her as she tries to pass to go to history class:

"Where did you get *those* shoes? Waaallll-Maaarrrttt? Oh . . . my . . . God!"

How can such a simple line from the mouths of little girls who look like baby Hillary Duffs carry so much venom, like they have just sprayed acid over this innocent girl who only wants to get to class?

I watch the girl with bad shoes melt, like the Wicked Witch, into the middle of the hall, and I know she will remember this day forever, just like the day I was told by a schoolmate that "little boys don't wear pink shirts. Little girls do."

Is it my role to say something, or not? I'm an administrator here, not a teacher. I stay silent because I fear the retribution, the rebuke, the attack that will surely follow from the Mean Mommies of the

Barbies. I have seen the Pink Ice Barbies' destruction, witnessed their hate, heard their words. I have seen the fire and brimstone that has rained down on the teacher who didn't give the Barbies the leads in the spring musical, the coach who didn't name all four to the varsity squad, or counselor who gave the girls copies of *The Hundred Dresses* to read and then tried to talk to them about the consequences of bullying and cliques.

I have seen too many good people taken down by bad ones, so I consciously decide to let this little girl with bad shoes take the abuse from the venomous offspring of these M²s just so I can avoid the crossfire.

The Size 4 Mary Janes
Are for Me, OK?

I am visited by the father of the little girl with *those* shoes. He is sitting in my office a few days later, waiting for me, stopping in early to see me before I even get a call from Kitsy. He is wearing a frayed, pilled navy blazer, with a T-shirt underneath. His short hair is flecked with gray, and his face is lined and tan. Though he is relatively young—late thirties maybe—he looks older than his years. He speaks quietly to me, looking around in a reverential way.

"It's harder than I thought," he says to me, "keeping up with everything."

I know immediately what he means by "everything."

"You need to talk to the admissions director, or the director of business," I say gently. "They can help you. This really isn't my area."

"I can't do that. I don't want anyone to see me walking into one of those offices. They'll know why. I was told to talk to you. That you'd understand . . . help me."

This isn't the first time a parent has come to me regarding the financial strain of attending Tate, even if they receive a generous financial aid package. Tate is exceedingly generous with its financial aid. The school believes in and wants a diverse school, knowing a wide range of people and experiences in the classroom and community helps define a great education. And Tate tells all families about "additional expenses," those that go "above and beyond the cost of tuition." Yet I'm sure it always comes as a shock to discover what above and beyond can truly mean: the right clothes, the right shoes, tutors, laptops, athletics, extracurriculars, field trips and, of course, just trying to keep up with the Joneses, some of whom are able to budget hundreds of dollars a month for manicures and blow-outs.

These financial aid families may attend Tate, but that doesn't mean, sadly, they can "keep up" at Tate. That doesn't mean they can go to Fiji or the Galapagos on spring break every year, or that their kids can attend the soccer camp at Stanford or the acting workshop in London, or that their kids get a $250 allowance each week, or that a sixteenth birthday automatically means a new Audi TT convertible. It's hard to be the only one who can't afford something in a world where most everyone can.

The father nervously unbuttons his blazer to reveal a navy blue T-shirt that says "Union Pipefitters: Local 157."

"I keep the blazer in my car for when I have to come into the school," he says apologetically. He takes a deep breath to calm himself but his lungs rattle and he starts coughing, hacking, a deep smoker's cough. "I'm so sorry. It's just that my little girl is so smart. She's just . . . so special, you know? God has truly blessed her . . . truly blessed me. And I want her to have everything I never had, to have only the best opportunities, no matter the cost. I want her to go here, I want her to go to a private college, and not work a blue-collar job. I want her to be one of these people. She just wants to fit in . . . I just want to fit in. I feel paralyzed."

I can feel my heart in my throat. I do not want to cry, and I am so close to breaking down right now. I want to say so much, but I don't.

I want to tell this good man that, unfortunately, this is really what it all comes down to at Tate and in life—embarrassment for never being good enough. No one can know that you receive financial aid, or that your grandparents pay your tuition, or that you're a hardworking blue-collar dad just trying to give his incredibly bright daughter the very best education he can, and a better life than he has.

No one can know that, even though you drive a new Jag and just moved into a $1.25 million home, you charge your monthly mortgage and your credit cards are nearly maxed.

No one can even know, for instance, that you are gay.

What all of this truly means, I believe, is that none of us ever feels good enough, especially in a world that places so much emphasis on perfection.

This is why the Saturday after talking with this father, when I am shopping at the mall, I beeline into Gap Kids instead of Banana Republic, my usual destination, and pick up the cutest pair of little girls' pink glitter ballet flats I have ever seen. I guess a size that I think will be appropriate, and head for the register, where the teenaged clerk who looks like Ashlee Simpson glares at me like I'm insane, her finger hovering just under the counter, over the security call button.

"They'll fit," I tell her like a crazy man, waving my debit card in front of her face.

On Monday I get to school extra early and secretly leave my gift in the locker of the girl with *those* shoes. There are no locks on many of the lockers—this is Tate, after all. After first period, I go into the hall to watch the kids changing class; I go into the hall to watch the little girl.

She has big green eyes, her daddy's jaw, and sandy hair, which is pulled back into a ponytail that flips around her head like a horse's tail. She wears little ruffly skirts nearly every day, tries so hard to look like the other little, rich girls. I look down at her feet. She is already wearing my shoes. They fit perfectly. They match her outfit perfectly.

She walks down the hall, head upright, a fresh touch of lip gloss, smiling brightly, her body filled with a world of confidence. She walks directly by the Barbies, not dawdling by her locker as usual, waiting for the clique to leave or disperse. For once, she does not have to care what they think, because she has nice shoes. She doesn't care where her flats came from; she's just thrilled that they have appeared from heaven, like a sparkly, pink shooting star.

I *know* this is not a smart thing for me to have done, because very soon she will scuff them or outgrow them, or the style will change, or her parents will call Tate to report this curious incident. I know this is not a smart thing to do because fashion does not make her a better person. I know this flies in the face of emphasizing the inside over the outside, but I just can't imagine her going through one more day in bad shoes, one more day being bullied by the Barbies.

No child should endure that. Not even for one day.

I buy these shoes for all the wrong reasons. To make myself feel better. To make up for everything I've never said or done.

I buy these shoes for all the right reasons, too. To let a child have some peace for a day. To buy a gift for a child who will never be my own. To buy a gift for a child who rarely gets girly little extras from her father but who I pray will realize one day everything her daddy has done for her.

Mostly, however, I buy these shoes to make up for everything I've never said or done.

Raise the Roof

Kitsy asks me to "chaperone" a small, private, off-campus student holiday dance with her following Thanksgiving. Though I know she really didn't want to come to this alone, embarrassed her husband is never with her, she instead tells me that it is important for me to take photos, for us to experience student life *together,* to connect with our future alumni.

If connecting means watching them make out and dance like Usher and Ashanti, I know that I am. I know that if I were a mommy, I wouldn't have let my child come to this dance without a bodyguard whose neck looks like a silo.

The dance is at a country club, which has a retractable roof on the dance pavilion that has been opened so the kids can dance under the stars. I didn't know roofs retracted. Mine recently opened at home, but that's because it collapsed. And I wasn't dancing as a result.

No, to be a popular student in the Upper School at Tate, I now understand, is like being Lindsay Lohan or Chris Klein. Every day is a pretty day. A magical day. At least on the outside.

I don't mean to overexaggerate, and I don't mean to overlook the fact that these kids are smart and driven, but most everyone does indeed look fabulous. Beyond fabulous, really, although the girls are barely dressed—in skin-tight tops and skirts. I don't know how the girls can even dance in them, much less how they managed to arrive here in the first place. I picture them walking here along the highway, slowly, in six-inch heels, or walking up a ramp, like cattle, and onto the back of a transport trailer, standing the whole way until they got dumped here.

The boys fall into one of two categories: They either look preppy, collars turned up, loose ties, unstructured jackets, or they look like they were just initiated into the Rich, White Boy Crips, gigantic jeans barely clinging to their bony hips, revealing boxers with gangsta slogans, Sean John jerseys and giant (real) gold chains bouncing into their concave chests. I love our thin, blond, white boys who think they are black, who think they are straight outta the hood, but actually look like they should be on *Laguna Beach*. I love hearing them blast rap music from their brand new Jeeps or mini-Hummers, standing by their possessions, talking about how their spinning silver hubcaps give them "street cred." I know for a fact that they have never been in the "'hood," could barely even ID the hood of their Hummers much less identify the 'hood on a map of our city. Part of me would like to dump their white asses in the 'hood for an evening, and see if they make it out intact, with their gold chains and pearly teeth.

I am staring at the crowd, semi-appalled and semi-impressed at the general state of affairs, all the kids either talking on cell phones, or making out quickly while they dance, or combining all of these elements in a bizarre, wealthy tribal ritual.

And then Kitsy looks at me, deeply, like Andrew McCarthy looked at Molly Ringwald at the end of *Pretty in Pink*, and asks me if I would like to dance.

I don't have a chance to respond "No," because she grabs my arms and drags me onto the floor, where she begins gyrating to

"Livin' La Vida Loca" by Ricky Martin. Kitsy is wearing a white Lilly Pulitzer candy island hut dress—a sleeveless dress that ties in the back, features little green palm trees and little pink cabanas along the bottom, and sets off her tan to perfection. I, on the other hand, am not moving. I am standing still and lifeless, watching my nemesis shake her groove thang, my soul fleeing, my spirit now hovering somewhere at the top of the pavilion ready to fly away into the night sky.

She maneuvers me toward the center of the floor, where I now see the Pink Ice Barbies all dancing together in a circle. "Oh, my God! Kitsy! Hi! Isn't this the best?"

Why are they even here? Their daughters aren't even here. Is this normal parental behavior? I have an uneasy feeling I will see them making out with some sophomore boys in the back of a mini-Hummer later tonight.

"I loved Tate!" Kitsy suddenly screams over the music. "I was everything here. I had so many friends. It was the best time of my life!"

I can relate, I think as I dance like Elaine from *Seinfeld*. I once wore an eggplant-colored corduroy suit to a formal and fake-slow-danced with a girl who once, on a dare, bench-pressed a goat. Yes, our school experiences were very similar. You were everything, and I was nothing. My dances looked like episodes of *Hee-Haw;* this looks like MTV staged a reunion party for the former castmates of *The Real World.*

I finally realize that Kitsy is staring at me staring at the crowd. She thinks I am impressed. She thinks I should be impressed.

"This place is amazing, huh? Just like my dances. I hope it never changes. I'm glad I've stayed involved at Tate. I just love being popular!"

And it is now that I realize: Things never change for Kitsy. Because they don't have to change for her. In this city, many of our wealthy citizens don't move, and outsiders don't stay. The grip of power that begins at birth never loosens its fist, holding tight until death. If you are not a part of this power structure from the start, you can never gain entrance.

This is what makes our city a boomerang city, where wealthy kids may leave for a short period of time—to attend an Ivy League college, or move for a first job—but always eventually return. The big bad world outside of here isn't, shockingly, always as wonderful as this little snow globe.

"I'm having a blast! Aren't you?" Kitsy asks me, her hips and legs a gyrating whir of pink and green, tiki huts, and palm trees.

I nod and look up at the open night sky, clouds beginning to cover the twinkling stars, a rumble of thunder in the distance. Some-one somewhere hits a button and the roof begins to close. I watch the two sides meet and clamp shut, and I wonder, *Will my roof make it through the storm? And whatever happened to the girl who bench-pressed that goat?*

Happy Holidays,
Homeless People!

"Tate PR Office. This is Wade."

"I need you to snag me eight cans of veggies, two pairs of children's shoes, three pairs of mittens, a scarf, stocking cap, and as many stuffed animals as you can carry, OK?"

It's 8:00 A.M. It's Kitsy. This is what happens when I think I am in the free and clear, when I think I have made it through a morning without having to make an appearance in carpool.

"I'm not sure I understand," I say. "You want me to steal donations for you?"

"It's not *stealing*, Wade! It's *borrowing!* I have holiday volunteer meetings all over town this morning, and I forgot to bring my donations. I was much too busy this morning to worry about all that fuss, so I need some 'loaners.' I can't drive around town empty-handed, can I? I mean, you wouldn't want me representing Tate looking like a pauper. How would that look? Carpool lane. TTFN!"

I sprint out of my office and down our hallway with my arms already loaded; the majority of conscientious students and parents have beaten the M²s to the punch and donated their goods on time. Since my office is a prime parent stopping point, it often serves as a temporary storage facility for much of this loot. Most M²s will scurry into my office at the very last minute carrying Ann Taylor bags stuffed with fluffy boas, or scuffed suede pants, or damaged high heels to donate to the homeless shelters. Because mothers and children living in the streets or in shelters need these things, need to look good for their charity events and Country Club dinners and jaunts to Vail.

I exit my office, arms filled. A corridor of windows running the length of our front hall looks out over the campus. Morning carpool is slowing but still in mid-chaos. A light snow is falling, blurring my view a little, making it look as if I am tinkering with the image in PhotoShop. And yet, out of all the fur-clad women riding high in their giant black Escalades, Excursions, and Navigators, I instantly see Kitsy. That's because LulaBelle is hanging out of the Land Rover's passenger window, despite the cold and the snow, sporting tiny reindeer antlers, a candy-cane-inspired collar, pink doggles, little pink Mutt-a-Luks, and a hot pink, fur-trimmed sweater that says, "Ho-Ho-Woof!" She looks like a transgendered Rudolph who has been run through the dryer on high heat one too many times.

Of course, Kitsy didn't have time to gather donations, but she did have time to dress LulaBelle for a day on the town.

Tate Academy places a huge emphasis on service-learning, what was known as community service when I was in school. In those days, I used to play with our school band at nursing homes, or give blood. The difference today is that the curriculum is inextricably tied to giving back—students learn about it in the classroom and then actually do it in the local community, for a one-two punch— such as studying about the effects of poverty in America and its toll on the nation, and then volunteering to build Habitat for Humanity homes alongside families who need them.

Each division at Tate coordinates its own effort. The Lower School puts up a monstrous Fraser fir in their tiled foyer that is decorated with kids' donations to families in need at the holidays. The tree is hung with mittens and socks and tiny shoes. The Middle School conducts a canned food drive in order to provide local shelters with much-needed supplies—mostly organic, natch—during the busy holiday season. And the Upper School collects gently used stuffed animals, which are given as gifts to families who can't afford to buy presents.

I coordinate the press coverage, each year trying to ensure that Tate looks like a Catholic School for the Blind, forgetting to include in my press releases or sound bytes that our organic food and couture donations would better be suited for feeding the Douglas-Zeta-Joneses, or clothing the Hiltons, if these families had suffered a down year. On one hand, I know that it's fine for people to buy gifts and simply drop them off—at least they are giving of their financial blessings—but wouldn't you think Kitsy—like the rest of us—might at least have a passing thought about the meaning behind all of this?

I am obsessed with this question as I begin to make my way down the snow-dampened front steps of our beautiful, columned building, my pockets stuffed with pesticide-free cans of peas and creamed corn, my hands juggling colorful giraffes and turtles, shiny shoes and striped mufflers stored in the crooks of my arms.

My vision and traction impaired by the snow, I mistakenly think the last step is the ground, and I begin to walk where there is still only air.

I fall. Hard. Throwing clothes and corn and kitties into the middle of carpool.

I fall. Hard. Directly into the fur-trimmed Uggs of the Barbies and their M^2s.

I have always, unfortunately, been a faller—off bicycles and skates, into fireplace hearths, down sidewalks and ladders. When I go down, I go down hard, tossing my coffee the length of the hallway, or flying headfirst down an escalator. It is the bad gene I inherited from a family who pulls hamstrings bowling or throws out their shoulders playing badminton. And so, once again, I find myself lying facedown on the ground, with no one coming to help me. The dueling quartet of older and younger Barbies simply flick their snow-flecked tresses over their fur-trimmed shoulders, giggle, and say, "Oh . . . my . . . God!"

I try to perform my yoga breathing exercises while prone, but inhale snow. So I push myself off the brick walkway, and dust myself off. I regather my menagerie of stolen contraband, and approach Kitsy's Land Rover.

She rolls down the passenger side window. "How embarrassing for you! Hurry!"

Kitsy pops the trunk, the sound of its opening serving as my instruction to drop the loot in the rear. I look into the back, and Mitsy smiles at me. LulaBelle pole-vaults over the seats, charging me like a baby bull in Pamplona. I slam the back door just as her cloth antlers strike the window.

And with that, Kitsy screeches off, turning the steering wheel like Jeff Gordon, performing a lightning quick U-turn in the middle of carpool, causing SUVs going in the right direction to screech to a halt. LulaBelle barks her disapproval at the other drivers, her antlers sliding down over her eyes. Kitsy heads toward the Lower School carpool to deposit Mitsy.

I walk back into the building, the reality of what I have just done starting to weigh on me. It may seem funny, it may seem insignificant, but what I have done is taken food from the mouths of people who truly need it, toys from children who won't get anything this year, shoes for kids living in shelters or on the streets, and regifted them to Kitsy to dole out cheerfully like Santa to über-rich organizations that are more likely to toss out the donations than hand them out.

Merry Christmas . . . and to all, a good night!

"Merry Christmas, Mrs. Rothstein!"

"Bring a torch, Jeanette, Isabella.
Bring a torch to the cradle, run!
It is Jesus, good folk of the village.
Christ is born and Mary's calling."

She is singing about Jesus? And, later, *he's* going to belt out a little ditty about Bethlehem?

I find this very amusing, in a cruel, Saturday Night Live–inspired way.

The voices of a Jewish girl and a Muslim boy singing Christmas songs. Belting out hymns in a darkened chapel. The spotlight silhouetting their bewildered faces. To a large crowd.

My job every holiday season is to help market an old, beloved, but wholly Christian celebration and Tate tradition to all our families, the Jews and the Muslims, the agnostics and atheists. This year, it must be a sellout, even if it means selling myself out.

And I do. With great success.

Still I seriously wonder, as I watch this boy and girl, if Kitsy has ever heard of Hanukkah or Kwanzaa. I'm sure she thinks Diwali is a perfume. I wonder if she knows that Jews simply think Christ is a super nice fella. Haven't we just gone through diversity and sensitivity training? I've even tried to ask her this, broach this sensitive subject, in my halting, gee-I'm-just-kinda-unsure sort of way.

"Who doesn't like Christmas and Santa, right? It's universal. I mean how could it not be?" she says to me, when I start to bring up my dilemma. "It's like chocolate. Everyone likes chocolate."

I had my answer.

So I market the hell out of our traditional festival of Christian psalms (reading of passages from the Bible) and Christian songs (a choir singing from hymnals), describing the evening to calling parents as an Old World celebration of the holidays, describing the event as akin to stepping into a Currier & Ives photo, with non-denominational carolers appearing at your frosted front door to sing songs of generic merriment.

It's brilliant, really.

And it works. We have a big house.

But, in reality, those who attend witness a throng of student singers enter a darkened chapel carrying candles, the light illuminating their white robes, eventually casting the stage in a glow, children's voices filling the air with songs about Jesus and Mary. They are joined onstage by members of the community who recite psalms and prayers about Christ from the Bible, the audience responding in unison.

It is all so beautiful. If you are Christian.

And so wrong if you aren't.

Because when I squint I can see the candles illuminating the faces of the families I feel I have duped, moms wringing their hands, fathers shifting back and forth, children who have no idea what is happening because these are not their customs, their beliefs. This is painful for me, because I am a Christian; this ceremony has meaning to me. But I am big enough to understand it doesn't for many, many others.

We could choose to have the kids sing "Let It Snow," or cute songs about reindeer and wassailing—like our youngest students do. We could even simply include Hanukkah or Kwanzaa songs in the program, truly celebrate one another's faiths, one another's uniqueness, have our students learn about diversity, have their minds changed and expanded, their beliefs and thoughts challenged by those who are different from them. This is a school, after all. That's what diversity is about, what real education means. Being challenged. Learning through someone else's eyes and experiences.

And still, I never receive a complaint. If they just stay quiet, I believe, this will work out in the long run, that they, too, will be part of the in-crowd, even though they celebrate seder or Kwanzaa.

They are just like me: desperately wanting to be accepted.

Kitsy Understands Me

Kitsy is staring at my left ring finger. It is naked.

My hand is clutching a clump of forgotten holiday programs, and my finger is exposed, perfectly displayed for inspection.

I do not wear a fake wedding ring, like some here do, trying desperately to pretend they are something they are not, who try to fake out the world, fool fate, terrified at every step that the curtain will finally be pulled off their charade, exposing them for who they are, like the Wizard of Oz. I have, at least, learned something from my struggle in coming out to my family and friends. I have a shred of honesty and self-respect embedded in me somewhere. Still, it is painful to live in this sterile environment every day, too easy to lie about myself.

Kitsy is still staring. She begins to purse her perfectly puffy lips.

Here it comes. The question. The one I dread. The one I am asked in classes and the cafeteria, at parent meetings and faculty lunches. The one I am asked by kids and adults. It doesn't matter who asks or when. It hurts every time, steals a bit of my soul each instance I have to lie.

No matter how much I expect it, anticipate it, the question always comes as a shock, like a firecracker whose fuse you think has already gone out, and then, Bam! It goes off. I will wander into a class to take a picture of a science experiment, and a girl will ask me, or I will sit down next to a teacher at lunch, and then I will go into my act, looking down shyly, shaking my head, saying, "Not yet. Maybe one day, I hope." And the girls will giggle, occasionally telling me about one of their moms, who is divorced. Or there's a sister. There's always a sister.

"Are you married?" Kitsy asks.

"No, I'm not."

Which is the truth. Sort of. I am not married. Not legally, of course, but in my eyes, the eyes of my family, friends, and God, I am joined with another, a person I love more than my life. So why can't I answer honestly? Is it because I'm afraid, or because I know I can't answer honestly here?

Be careful, I hear Cookie Henderson say. *Watch the lions.*

Kitsy eyes me over. But she doesn't offer up a divorced friend, or a sister. She is too smart. She simply looks at me—up and down, and down and up—with those piercing blue eyes, which right now are registering pity and hatred and sadness and revulsion and confusion.

But then she smiles at me, sweetly, sadly.

"I am," she says, laughing, breaking the tension. And then she adds, "You'd make a wonderful father. My daughter thinks you are so sweet."

My heart simultaneously breaks and overflows.

I do not understand this woman. Just when I think she is despicable, subhuman, she seems to see me for the very first time, seems to thaw, seems to have a heartbeat, seems to actually know me. I love children. I tell myself I took this job to be in with the ultimate in-crowd, but I know, deep inside, that I really took it to be around kids, to help children in some, minute way.

Perhaps, I think, Kitsy really does like me.

Angry Errand Boy

No, she just *needs* me.

It is tradition at Tate Academy to close for two full weeks at the holidays. This gives students and faculty a breather from the rigors of our academic calendar.

In reality, the two-week break is also a societal requirement at Tate in order for some families to enjoy two completely different week-long vacations—one cold and one warm.

For Kitsy, this means traveling to Door County, Wisconsin, for a week to spend time at her family cottage on the lake to cross-country ski and snowshoe and roast marshmallows over a roaring fire and watch Mitsy build snowmen. This is the Christmas part of the holiday. The second part kicks off with a trip to Naples, Florida, where Kitsy can officially launch her yearlong tanning season and so the family can spend time in a beach environment, golfing, sunbathing, playing tennis, searching for shells. This is the New Year's part of the holiday. "We like to be someplace Christmas-y, and then someplace beach-y, don't you? I can't imagine it any other way," Kitsy command-asks me like I've just crawled from the center of the earth and am learning the customs of normal Americans.

Yes, I want to reply. *I, too, like to take vacations in two different, exotic locales, which is why Gary and I spend time with our families in rural America, where even the cattle look bored.*

But many Tate families do perform this exotic vacation tango, splitting time between Aspen and Phoenix, or Montana and Cabo. A similar thing happens at spring break, too, with families spending the first week jetting off to a warm, exotic destination and the second week "officially" reopening their cottages for the summer.

For some reason, the success or failure of Kitsy's multiple vacations has somehow landed squarely on my shoulders, which I guess are just barely wider than those of Lilly, who is also traveling, and less hunched than those of Kitsy's maid, Clementine. I know I *should* set some boundaries. I know I *should* report this. I know the school doesn't expect me to do this, and that I *should* immediately go to Doty to discuss my dilemma, but, deep down, I am worried he would tell me I *should* easily be able to "squeeze it in if I manage my time well," and that "a little extra attention isn't really uncalled for."

I know I do this to please her.

So I spend an entire week in mid-December helping send Louis-Vuitton-crammed bags of pink snowsuits and snowshoes and furry boots and cute tasseled stocking caps to Kitsy's cottage in Door County and then another set of Louis-Vuitton-crammed bags of pink Lilly Pulitzer swimwear and sandals and sarongs and summer dresses along with sets of golf clubs and tennis rackets to Naples.

I tell Kitsy—with a bizarre sense of pride—when I am done. I imagine her being so blown away with my packing and FedExing skills, that she will surprise me with a trip somewhere warm, or, at the very least, another belt.

"Did you put Wearing History tags on each clothing item?" she instead asks casually at the coffeehouse when I tell her I have successfully completed the task that should not have been mine to begin with.

I hear tires screeching, brakes squealing, me being thrown head first through the front of my Toyota Corolla.

"Do what, when, what?" I stutter.

"Wearing History tags, Wade! All of my clothes *must have* tags attached so I can mark when I wore what and where I wore it. I can't imagine being caught in the same outfit twice, right? Isn't that what you do? Isn't that what everyone does?"

Actually, I want to tell her, my heart racing from the stress and caffeine, I don't know how anyone on this planet can even discern one of her pink outfits from the next. And, furthermore, I cram sweats and oversized hooded sweatshirts into a backpack when I visit our families over the holidays, because the only places I will be going are to bed, the couch, the bathroom, or the fridge either to sleep, poop, or eat something that has Velveeta, Ritz crackers, or chocolate chips in it.

Our holidays are not the same. By a long shot.

And why weren't these tag things mentioned in the first place? This is *not* common knowledge among people who make less than $2 million a year.

I leave in a panic and immediately run to see the FedEx guy, who looks like Matt Damon. I beg him to ship all of Kitsy's bags back to me, which he orchestrates by yawning and pushing buttons on a computer screen. The bags are redelivered, and I unpack everything and place Wearing History tags on every single thing that can be worn. I debate about tagging her pink panties but ultimately decide if she can't remember what underwear she just wore then that's her problem.

When I finally get a few precious hours to do my Christmas shopping, I am grumpy, exhausted, and hateful, like I'm Santa and just walked in to find Mrs. Claus sleeping with both Donner and Blitzen.

Over the course of an hour, these are the God's-honest-truth actual conversations I have as I cram in errands that I haven't gotten to do for weeks because I've been serving as Kitsy's elf.

To the Banana Republic clerk who looks just like Justin Timberlake: "You don't have gift boxes? How is that possible at this time of year? Please enlighten me. Yes, I want my receipt. Jesus, it's just like watching Jonas Salk at work."

To the Colin Farrell wannabe at the Gap: "Do you have a size thirty-two? Could you look in the back? Typically, the back is in the back of the store. That's what I thought. It's amazing what you can find when you actually stop air-spiking your hair and assist a customer. TTFN!"

I have so much unresolved anger at work, I find myself taking it out on anonymous retail clerks and grocery store checkers and waiters; I think since they will never see me again, that it's OK.

But it's not. Because, subconsciously, I begin to think that I am better than these hourly workers are, that they need to do what I say when I say it.

I am really no better than the women I despise.

I'm devolving. I have never been this intentionally mean and angry. I never take out my problems on others.

And now I find myself taking it out on part-time workers. And Gary.

"You need to be happy," he says. "You need to find your smile."

"Did you just see *City Slickers* again? Thanks for your self-help bullshit. That'll do me a lot of good today. At least you can walk out into the world and be who you are, be honest with your coworkers, not hide who you are."

"We all have to be different at work," Gary says.

"Straight people don't have to pretend to be gay all day. Rich people don't have to pretend to be poor."

"Oh, give up the drama, Mr. Bitter. You cannot let these people have this much control over your life. It's killing you, and it's starting to kill me."

"Thanks, Oprah. I appreciate the help."

"I'm just saying that you'd better change your life, or you'll end up like them. I don't want anger in this house twenty-four-seven. We only get one shot at life, you know? You're a smart guy. Start acting like one."

The Grinch Shows Her Heart

Kitsy is on her third glass of Merlot. She is wearing a pink cashmere turtleneck and a gray cigarette skirt. She is sitting in a leather wingback chair in her study, next to a roaring fire. The fireplace has a hand-carved mantel, over which is hung an oil painting of Kitsy's family. They all look pretty. But sad. Even LulaBelle.

The whole scene makes me feel like I'm watching an episode of one of those very depressing dramas on the BBC.

Kitsy's face is flushed, the color of her wine, and her hair looks fake in the fire's light, overprocessed, overbleached, staticky white strands backlit and standing on end, like she's just shuffled her feet on carpet and touched metal. I can see her collarbones jutting out under her turtleneck, and her stomach looks concave. Her left leg is crossed over her right, and she nervously twirls her foot—fast, fast, faster—until her spike heel looks like a whirring beater in a blender.

Kitsy looks at me and tries to smile. It is too much of an effort.

Right now, Kitsy looks sad. And tired. And frail. Like a hologram of her real self. For once, Kitsy doesn't look perfect.

I am nervous and uncomfortable. I have made her one-dimensional in my mind, to laser my hate on her rather than myself. She is 3-D flesh and blood right now, and I don't like it. I don't like it at all.

She asked me over to her residence ostensibly to discuss how to improve the holiday program, while the event was still fresh in our minds. Now, however, I realize she is lonely, that she has asked me over just because she needs somebody to talk to. I really think that she wants to know more about me, but that she has forgotten how to reach out to anyone anymore. Her only remaining human emotions are greed, sarcasm, manipulation, superiority—not good ones to have when you're in trouble and need a real friend.

I had tried to get out of this dinner date for a week, thinking of elaborate excuses to extricate myself from this very moment, where she looks at me, stares at me, like I'm her *Knot's Landing* left-for-dead husband who has survived the boat capsizing to return from the dead.

Kitsy talks half-heartedly about the holiday program, but she offers no "grand ideas" tonight, does not seem up to outdoing herself.

There is a giant grandfather clock in the corner of the study, its big brass pendulum swinging back and forth, like a metronome on top of a piano. Kitsy nervously checks the time every few minutes. I am watching her closely, but she thinks I am admiring the clock.

"My grandparents had it made in Switzerland. I've always loved it, the sound of the seconds ticking away, the chimes . . ." She drifts away for a moment. She is somewhere else. And then she asks, "Did you have a nice childhood?"

Besides asking me if I was married, she has never asked a question about my life before, never desired to know anything except for my cell phone number. "I did," I say, not wanting to delve into the real details of my life.

"I didn't," Kitsy says. "I mean I was popular, but school was like work. I was expected to be popular, to achieve. I never got to be a kid.

I was just a mini-adult, achieving things my parents wanted me to achieve. I didn't even get to jump rope. I didn't even . . . get hugged."

She says this slurrily, and then drifts off again. I pretend to stare at the fire, until my pupils start to burn. I can't stand the silence, so I say, "My family always hugged. My Grandma Shipman always said, 'Hugs are for free. I may not be able to give you material things, but I can always give you a hug, let you know how much you are loved. And that will make you a very rich man.' "

Kitsy locks eyes with me and stiffens. "How quaint," she says with a tone of arrogance. "Are you still close with John Boy and Mary Ellen?"

"It's not quaint, and that's not remotely funny," I answer, the words coming out testy and tense. "Love isn't quaint. It's family. That's what families do. Support one another, even when you fail, even when you're not everything you think your parents want you to be."

I am instantly embarrassed by my tone and again look into the fire. Kitsy follows my eyes to the flames and softly says, "I'm sorry. I didn't mean it to come across that way."

This is the first and only apology I will ever get from her.

"I . . . I . . . I tend to push people away before they get too close. I'm used to people leaving," she says. "I'm used to people lying. I'm used to people being mean. I'm used to people who can only be sarcastic and demeaning. That's my world."

And it is now that I begin to understand her, begin to see the roots of what has made her the person she is today.

Kitsy nervously checks the clock again. Tick. Tock. Tick. Tock.

"You asked me once about our business. My husband and I didn't even really need to start our own business. We didn't really need the money, you know? But we wanted to make our marks in the world, not simply be known as trust-fund kids. We had an agreement, my husband and I. We'd make our mark, and then make our family, the way we wanted it to be. We'd be parents. Our children would be able to be kids."

She looks at the clock. She is talking to the clock now. "We made a pact. But success begs for more success. Doing it one time might be seen as a fluke, you know? So my husband wants to do it all over again. We don't have to work, but he doesn't know anything else. He has to trump his parents. They had to trump their parents. He has to trump his friends. We must have more than our friends. Work . . . can be such an excuse. But we don't really have options in life, do we?"

She stops. For a second, her foot stops twirling, and her head sinks. She is just white hair on top of pink cashmere. She is as fragile as cotton candy, ready to disintegrate with just the slightest touch of moisture.

Kitsy is right. And wrong. Work can be an excuse in life, filling our emptiness, our hours, until it is 2:30 P.M. on the office clock thirty years later, and we've never really addressed anything, meetings replacing decisions, returning phone calls and e-mails replacing hope and fear and motivation and inspiration.

But we all have options. We just need the courage to follow them.

With that, I hear padded footsteps, and Mitsy runs through the door wearing pink-footed pj's, skidding to a stop when she sees me. This is Kitsy's option. Why can't she see it?

"Hi, Mr. Rouse. Merry Christmas."

"What do you have there?" I ask about the paper she's holding.

"Our teacher asked us to draw our favorite thing about the holidays."

"What'd you draw, sweetie?" Kitsy asks.

"You and daddy and LulaBelle."

Kitsy takes the drawing and studies it closely. "It's beautiful, sweetie." She reaches out and pats her daughter, and, for the first time, I see the essence of a good person in there, a good mother.

Where does this person go every morning? I think, *Why does she have to hide?*

And then I hear LulaBelle barking, and a door slam. It is Kitsy's husband. It is 9:30 P.M., and he's just getting home from work.

"No dinner?" I hear her husband yell from the kitchen. "Where's Clementine?"

Kitsy sent her maid home two hours ago, when dinner ended and her husband still hadn't called.

His frame enters the door. You can feel his ego fill the room long before.

"Mitsy, you should be in bed. What the hell am I going to eat?" He now notices I am in the room. "We have guests?"

"A guest," Kitsy says. "You remember Wade Rouse, who I work with closely at Tate. I invited him over to talk about the holiday program. You were supposed to join us for dinner."

"It's nice to meet you," he says to me. We have met at least twenty times before.

"Well . . ." he says, staring at me.

It's my cue to go.

"It's late. I'd better go. I'm sorry to keep you so long."

"I'll walk you to the door." Kitsy stands unsteadily and smooths her skirt, before saying coldly to her husband, "Your dinner is in the refrigerator."

"I'm not hungry anymore. Jesus, are we even ready to leave town? What did you do all day?" he says angrily but distantly, like he's calling from a cell phone with bad reception, and yelling at an American Airlines reservationist about his flight delay. "I've got more work to do. I'll be in my office."

He begins to depart, grabbing Mitsy brusquely by the hand.

"Bye, Mr. Rouse," she says. "Hey? Are you OK?"

This has become our routine. She always asks if I'm OK.

"I'm great," I say. "How 'bout you?"

She shrugs, and her dad drags her away, her padded feet skidding along the way.

Kitsy walks me to the door. We pass from room to room to room to room, tile turning to stone to hardwood to Berber. Her residence is decorated like the White House for the holidays, lights and trees twinkling and reflecting, illuminating expensive antiques and artwork as we pass, illuminating yet another Liza-inspired mountain of luggage piled in the front foyer, but mostly illuminating the sadness and emptiness of this mini-mansion.

At her mammoth front door, I thank Kitsy for having me to her home. "It's so beautiful," I say. "You have amazing taste."

I don't know what to say, really.

"I'm sad," she says, slurrily. "I mean, tired. I'm tired. I kept you too long. I'm sorry."

I have no idea what comes over me, but I reach in to hug Kitsy, to give her the hug she never had as a child, that she will never get as an adult, to hug this woman I have never really seen, to make sure she's real. And she is. She hugs me back, holding me tightly. This gesture scares and overwhelms me.

"Thank you," she says, and then she laughs suddenly and out of the blue asks, "Do you know why I call you *Señor Mantequilla?*" She pushes me back and holds me at arm's length, holding onto my shoulders as though she might shake me at any minute. "Because I can't joke with anyone in my life. No one has a sense of humor. Everyone is very serious, all of the time. I came from serious parents and I married a serious man and all my friends are serious.

"He's not in my league, you know? I mean financially he is, but not . . ."

Her voice trails off, and her lower lip quivers, like a scared kid who doesn't want to cry. She battles her sadness, smiles wanly, and says, "I think you are funny. And sweet. You're different. I just can't put my finger on it. But I like you. I like you very much, *Señor Mantequilla*."

I am dumbfounded. And sweating. I feel like I'm simultaneously melting and sinking into quicksand.

"I'd better get to bed. We're heading to our cottage in Door County tomorrow for the holidays. But you know that already. I'm sorry."

I do. I sent all your luggage, remember? Instead I say:

"Thanks for having me into your home. Have a wonderful holiday."

She nods and shuts the giant door on her giant house.

I drive home to my tiny bungalow; my whole house is smaller than Kitsy's study.

Gary is watching a Lifetime movie, where Jo from *The Facts of Life* has been raped and is fighting back against her attacker.

"Girl, Jo's in trouble," Gary says when I walk in the door. "Are you?"

"I'm OK," I say, though I go in for the one hug I've really needed all night.

Of course, Kitsy and I never talk about our night together. It's like it never happened. In two weeks, I will be her employee once again, her little lackey.

And even though I still feel intimidated by her, I now feel sorry for her.

That night I dream that I am mired in quicksand in Kitsy's study. The fire is roaring, the room looks the same as it did when I was there. Just as I am about to go under, to sink under the muck, Kitsy comes to life in the portrait hanging over the fire, and extends her perfectly manicured hand to help me. When I'm about to take hold of her tanned hand, she draws it back and scratches in the quicksand with her long, French manicured nail: "I'm sinking, too."

As I go under, I take one final glance at the portrait. The family still looks sad. Even LulaBelle.

Word Power

During the holidays, Tate's campus finally becomes still and quiet. My phone stops ringing, I cease my morning yoga chanting, I don't have to make the trek to carpool for a few weeks.

However, I still go to check on Miggie because I know she has nowhere else to go, nowhere else to be. So I spend time reading her some of my favorite books, like *The Catcher in the Rye,* and even more modern favorites of mine like *Bonfire of the Vanities* or *Less Than Zero.* She likes these, understands from being at Tate so long the books' sad undertexts.

However, when it is Miggie's turn to pick a book, she always and only has one request: *Wuthering Heights.*

"It was my favorite book as a teen. It still is," she says. I read from her childhood copy, whose spine is loose and crooked, whose pages are thin and crinkly, the book's physical attributes now matching those of its owner. Some days, as I read, Miggie will begin to cry softly and think of something—lost love, a life gone too fast—her eyes fixed on a point on the wood floor, her mind light-years away.

And so I keep reading, like a teacher to a child, my voice trying to calm her, the words from *Wuthering Heights* still haunting her, the words now haunting me:

Heathcliff had knelt on one knee to embrace her; he attempted to rise, but she seized his hair, and kept him down.

"I wish I could hold you," she continued bitterly, "till we were both dead! I shouldn't care what you suffered. I care nothing for your sufferings. Why shouldn't you suffer? I do! Will you forget me? Will you be happy when I am in the earth? Will you say twenty years hence, 'That's the grave of Catherine Earnshaw. I loved her long ago, and was wretched to lose her; but it is past. I've loved many others since: my children are dearer to me than she was; and at death, I shall not rejoice that I am going to her: I shall be sorry that I must leave them!' Will you say so, Heathcliff?"

When I pause, I look up and over at Miggie, who has fallen asleep. Tears still wet her slackened cheeks, the grey whales on her navy blue scarf looking as if they've just blown salty sea foam onto her tired, old face.

I quietly open the Christmas gift she has gotten me. It is a DVD of *The Wizard of Oz.*

"Maybe this will help you remember how easy it is to find your courage, just like the Lion," her card says.

I smile, watching the old broad sleeping from my wooden rocker, her snoring in perfect synchronization with the squeaks of my chair as it rocks back and forth, and back and forth.

Part Two

The Spring Semester

"My mother and I are sitting in a restaurant on Melrose, and she's drinking white wine and still has her sunglasses on and she keeps touching her hair and I keep looking at my hands, pretty sure that they're shaking. She tries to smile when she asks what I want for Christmas. I'm surprised at how much effort it takes to raise my head up and look at her. *Nothing,* I say. There's a pause and then I ask her, *What do you want?* She says nothing for a long time and I look back at my hands and she sips her wine. *I don't know. I just want to have a nice Christmas.* I don't say anything. *You look unhappy,* she says real suddenly. *I'm not,* I tell her. *You look unhappy,* she says, more quietly this time. She touches her hair, bleached, blondish, again. *You do, too,* I say, hoping that she won't say anything else. She doesn't say anything else, until she's finished her third glass of wine and poured her fourth."

—Clay, *Less Than Zero,* by Bret Easton Ellis

Cowardly Courageous Conversations

"Thank you. I appreciate your concern, but I am going to walk away now from this conversation until you are able to speak civilly to me. Good day."

I start the second semester at Tate not with my typical Zen-inspired yoga chanting to center myself, but rather with the verbal swords and narrative daggers I so desperately need to fend for myself in the Tate Academy jungle of Mean Mommies.

I was doing it all wrong, you see.

Every January, Tate's administration selects an educational theme for the final semester, one that will inspire faculty and staff to finish the year strong and with conviction.

That's why I find myself this cold, blustery morning in one of our auditoriums attending a seminar called "Courageous Conversations." This is the hot new thing at Tate, the big idea in the world of education. Big ideas in education roll in moment by moment, it seems, like the tide. Yet, this is the very latest, the educational concept—like single-sex classes, or meta-cognition—that will transform our very lives from this day forward, make our school a virtual nirvana, turn each and every one of us into Gandhi.

Our seminar is being led by a very important educational and psychological consulting firm. The goal today is to provide faculty, staff, and administrators with the mediating skills and conversational tools to handle difficult confrontations with angry parents. Rather than taking their bait, we are being taught to diffuse the situation.

"You may call me at eight A.M. tomorrow when cooler heads prevail. I appreciate your concern for (your child, Tate, this event, etc.). Good day."

I am parroting this to a teacher, like I would to Kitsy, or Chachi, or the Pink Ice Barbies, readying myself for when they next ask me to do something with which I am not comfortable. Play-acting and memorization will allow me instantaneously to recall these magical words, you see, and stand against them with conviction—like a male Erin Brockovich—until calmer heads prevail.

Yet I realize that for some reason I have adopted a slight British accent as I say this. Perhaps it is a coping mechanism, or my own way of making fun of this nonsense, but I sound a bit like David Niven rehearsing a line in a play. I also sound like a fraud. I know that if I uttered this to Kitsy, she would command-ask my backside, or that if I repeated this to the Pink Ice Barbies, they would "Oh, my God!" me into oncoming traffic in carpool.

I want to ask these consultants how you really tell someone "no" who has never been told "no" in her entire life? Who has never been denied a single thing?

It's like holding a Bonz dog treat over a wild jackal and expecting it to sit when you say "sit." You know it's just going to rip your arm off instead.

I quickly grow bored with the presentation and drink way too much coffee to stay awake. Then, out of the blue, I am asked to play-act an angry parent-teacher confrontation. I am paired with a teacher—a method actor, of course—who is selected to play the parent. When we take our places, the teacher playfully pushes me out of anger, to simulate a real scenario. But I am not expecting this. I am, instead, concentrating so completely on controlling my bladder, that, when she pushes me, I fall down hard and tinkle a little in my pants. I rush out of the auditorium, sprinting to the bathroom.

"Fabulous! Fabulous simulation!" is the last thing I hear the consultant screaming into her lavalier mic. "Wade? Wade? Hello? Are you coming back?"

Not today, I think to myself. *Not today.*

The Ghost of Christmas Ass

I am late to work this January Wednesday not only because of the smattering of ice our city has on its roads, but also because I have to purchase Kitsy's special chicken salad, organic bread, and assortment of fruit teas from Gourmet-in-a-Go. I remember that we are also low on relaxation candles, so I segue into Pier 1 hoping Kitsy won't notice they are fakes, that they aren't really from the Asian market she frequents only twice a year in advance of one of her parties, when she needs these candles or her funny fortune cookies (she writes people's fortunes for them, and the market bakes them into the cookies; I'm convinced mine would say, "Pink is *now* your signature color").

Today, Kitsy is hosting an M^2-only get-together to talk about "school issues"—though she calls it "Chit-Chat over Chicken Salad," which is code for "gossip about everyone and make Wade's life a living hell for two hours." The event is a big draw, something, for some reason, I wasn't really anticipating, and, because of my tardiness and in my haste to make everything perfect for Kitsy and Company, I forget to check, as scheduled, on Miggie.

Until a staff member comes sprinting into the conference room, screaming, "Miggie's loose!"

I am elbow deep in chicken salad, arranging grapes in fruity question marks on top of the meaty, dilly, low-fat mayo-y concoction. Kitsy has told me to add this grape punctuation "to encourage chit-chat and lots of questions." I feel like the gay love child of Lynne Truss and Wolfgang Puck.

"And no one else can handle this?" I ask.

My coworker smiles. "She only listens to you, Wade. She loves you."

"Can you finish this and then start lighting the relaxation candles?"

I sprint out of the conference room and across campus, peering down hallways for the escaped convict. I feel like I should be in *Cagney and Lacey.* And then I hear it: girlish shrieks and boyish gasps of horror. I sprint to the science wing, an addition at the far end of the building, following the screams. I round the corner and there I see Miggie, her plaid skirt pulled up to her waist, her panties around her ankles, her bare ass pressed against the glass panes of a classroom. She is mooning a science class. Kids see more up close on this morning than they ever will peering through their microscopes.

She smiles when she sees me. "Two little girls asked me in the ladies' room if I were a ghost. I thought I'd let them decide for themselves."

"I think you're just a little confused this morning. Come with me, sweetie. You've still got a great butt, but I'm not sure this is the right viewing audience for it."

She laughs. I pull her skirt down and escort her back to my office.

"A ghost!" she says, clinging to my arm. "Can you imagine being so insolent? In my day, we would have had our mouths washed out with lye soap."

"Times are changing, aren't they?" I say softly. I make her some Folger's, microwave her a muffin and try to settle her down. "And what is lye exactly? Any way, I can't imagine you ever needing your mouth washed out."

I notice that she is watching me closely, in what looks like a rather confused state, like my grandfather used to do. *My friend is aging quickly, I think.*

I stop, look over at her and smile.

But then she says, clearly: "You're too good for this place. They'll eat you alive eventually."

"I've heard that before," I say. "From Cookie Henderson."

"I just love that woman. We've been around the block together a few times. And she's right, you know." Then, she says, without warning, "Do you have someone in your life?"

I feel like a gun has been fired. My heart is racing. I feel faint. I am, for once, unable to say a word.

I have nowhere to hide anymore. And so, for once, I tell the truth. "Yes. His name's Gary. We've been together for years."

"Dear Lord, boy. You should be shouting that from the mountaintops."

I laugh, relieved, but she turns serious.

"It's dangerous to be one of the few good people in a sea of bad ones. And I'm including myself in that mix. Remember that. Life goes too fast. You need to be happy in your life and work. You need to be open. You need to be loved. Simple stuff, really, but it makes all the difference."

Her words stick with me, scare me a little. I try to tell myself that she is just an old lady. But I also know that she has more clarity than I do. Age and a broken heart will give that to a person.

Your Tiara Is Distracting Me

Some days the schism between where I grew up and where I now work seems as wide as Kitsy's SUV.

Today, Tate is holding a "hat day" for students as a way to deal with its heated dress code issue. Or, rather, lack of dress code.

Of course, like any private school, Tate Academy has dress requirements: Tate students cannot wear jeans, or T-shirts, or sweatshirts. Boys must wear khakis or cords and a collared shirt or turtleneck. Once a week, on Mondays, Tate has formal dress day, where boys wear blue blazers and gold ties with Tate's crest, and girls wear long skirts or appropriate dresses. However, the rest of the week, it gets downright dicey when it comes to the way the girls dress—or don't dress. Girls can wear nearly anything, or nearly nothing at all, which is what some do: skirts so short they can't sit in class, tops that plunge more dramatically than a rollercoaster, open-toed shoes in the dead of winter. Tate is like a training school for high-class call girls. We have long discussed mandatory uniforms, but that will never fly at Tate. Parents here feel it removes good decision-making opportunities for children. But do they even see how their kids look before they leave every morning? And, if so, why don't they do anything to stop it?

That's why I shouldn't be surprised, really, that on Hat Day some

Tate girls show up wearing tiaras instead of baseball caps or cowboy hats. No, that shouldn't be surprising, considering our girls wear pearls and diamonds as often as rubber Lance Armstrong or friendship bracelets.

Still, this ostentatious display is always jarring for me, considering I went to school in a faux barn, a place that looked as if it might be where smart animals would go, a school for gifted cows, or musically inclined sheep, or goats that could speak three languages.

And it certainly smelled like a barn. Most days, even if the plumbing had not overflowed, the school's floors were covered in a layer of cow excrement or chicken crap, which coated the peel-and-stick as it fell off the Dingo boots of the farm kids (or "goat ropers," as I called them) following their early-morning chores. The floor was like a scratch-and-sniff; each time you took a new step, the odor would reintensify. Tate Academy, on the other foot, always smells like floor wax, expensive perfume, and fresh-cut flowers.

My school had little or no dress code. Kids wore cowboy hats and John Deere caps in class, tattered jeans and dirty T-shirts. In a bizarre twist of fate, I was the only one I knew in high school who ever got sent to the office for a dress code violation. The boy who dressed like the forgotten member of Wham! every day actually got in trouble for not wearing socks with his deck shoes.

"Do you have eyes?" I asked my interrogator, who was wearing suspenders, Dickies and a short-sleeved white dress shirt with giant yellow stains in the armpits. "I can't wear socks with these. It's just . . . wrong," I sputtered.

That's why it would seem that letting Tate students dress down, dress like normal kids, like public school kids, might take some of the competition out of dressing.

Tate has, for decades, endured "competitive dress," a term that is now part of the school lexicon. This fashion frenzy started decades ago, with girls trying to outdress each other for May Day, having their white dresses custom made. It turned into an all-out war, I was told, in the eighties, when Tate was listed as one of the preppiest schools in America. Tate tried to slow this fashion freight train down, but its efforts to enforce a real dress code were only half-hearted. Hemlines and heels just kept going higher, while necklines and the ability of young male teachers to ignore them dipped dramatically lower. Today, many Tate students look like Disney World versions of whores and thugs—glittered cleavage and tight, short skirts, untucked shirttails and gangsta-wannabe pants. Every day looks like a casting call for a new Lindsay Lohan movie or Puff Daddy video. It's hard to enforce a dress code when many M^2s dress just like their daughters. It's hard to enforce a dress code when there is an all-out war to dress more expensively, or fashionably, or revealingly than your best friend. Everything at Tate, even clothes, must be a competition.

That's why girls begin spilling out of their SUVs this morning looking like they are contestants in the Miss America pageant. To my shock, the crowns and tiaras a few of the girls wear are real—studded, coated, encrusted with actual diamonds; these are tiaras that were worn by their mothers in beauty contests or family heirlooms that have been passed down through the generations.

I try not to gape too much at this *Dynasty* revival. I clamp my jaw and do my job, taking pictures of girls in diamond-encrusted crowns playing Frisbee, drinking Diet Cokes, and taking notes on their laptops and tablets, like this is all completely normal.

Still, I guess I cannot shake my look of absolute bewilderment, because when I return to the office, I call Cookie Henderson and tell her about this. She tells me—like she's telling a child from Manhattan that milk actually comes from cows—"Honey, those are the only hats they have."

And I accept this as normal, too—just as I did the hundreds of kids I went to school with who wore cowboy hats the size of flying saucers, chewed Skoal and spit their black saliva onto the back legs of my new Calvin Kleins as I went to class. Of course, girls wearing tiaras is normal. What is normal anyway? Certainly, out of all the people in this world, I am not the best judge.

Mommy, Why's the Lunch Lady a Man in a Two-Foot-Tall Chef's Hat?

I am scratching my head, which is itchy and sweaty, both out of physical necessity and out of complete bewilderment as to how I found myself here, right now, in my latest plight, standing alone wearing a giant chef's hat and serving Tater Tots.

In an attempt to put in motion an initiative that actually supports what we say in our mission statement, a few M²s actually put forth an effort I think is capable of tying our community together, like a beautiful quilt.

I am such a Pollyanna, without the cool name.

Kitsy suggests to me on behalf of the group that we all help serve lunch to their kids. The goal, I believe, is to give our hardworking food service staff a break, to show them that we actually appreciate their efforts in cooking, cleaning, and mopping up rich kids' peas and Kool-Aid for a few bucks an hour, to show that we are all really one big, happy family.

And we are. It's just that we're the Ozzy Osbournes. We're rich, but more than a bit dysfunctional.

Which is why I have been standing mostly alone for the past two hours in a hairnet and two-foot-tall chef's hat, serving Manwiches,

Tater Tots, corn, and chocolate brownies. This was supposed to be a day where we all worked together, which is why I guess the M²s are all sitting at a large table drinking Tab and eating cubed pieces of apples, cucumber, and melon, all of which looks like it should be sitting in the bottom of a gerbil cage.

I have many unanswered questions, the first of which is: *They still make Tab?*

Yes, I somehow delusionally dreamed that the mommies would mingle with the food service staff, eat with them, get to know them. Yet, the reality is that the men and women who work in the cafeteria are all crammed into a tiny round table in the corner, like they've been quarantined.

Only one mommy—Riffie, the leader of the Pink Ice Barbies—has even bothered to introduce herself to the staff, and that simple task is a disaster.

"Hello, *Hola* and Whassup?" Riffie had "shouted out" jokingly to her homies, some of whom are either black or Bosnian. I'm sure she thinks they are all just tan. "*Me llamo* is Riffie."

I watch this scene filled with horror and amusement and pity, for everyone involved, including me. Part of me wants to see a few of these cooks and dishwashers grab her, hold her ninety-five-pound body down and stuff the yellow gold pin in the shape of a banana that she is wearing up her newly reconstructed nose while screaming, "Lunch is served!" Part of me simply wants to flip Manwich meat into her blond bob. But no one, of course, does anything, except smile and nod, even me, trying to politely pantomime a look of happiness for the group. The seated M²s whisper and stare at us with complete bemusement, like they're on safari and watching wild jungle animals cavort from the safety of their Jeep.

At least, from my end, no one has really eaten that much for lunch, making my job a breeze. All the girls simply beelined to the salad bar, or the cereal canisters, or soft-serve ice cream machines to ingest the few calories that will keep them upright through PE and field hockey practice and lacrosse matches.

Kitsy catches my pained expression as I scratch my head, and she not-so-subtly grabs my attention from her seat at the table. She takes her tanned, manicured index finger and traces a smile across her face, reminding me to be HAPPY! And then she blows a kiss at me and yells, "Nice hat!"; the mommies dying, absolutely dying in laughter, at the lunch table, just like I'm sure they did in seventh grade at whatever poor slob happened to fall into their radar. I'll bet they're even sitting at their favorite table in exactly the same seats.

A half-hour later, on her way out, Kitsy checks in with me and says, "What a great idea. Tell everyone we're in for next year, OK?"

The mommies all depart, following Kitsy like a flock of geese in a V, cackling, quacking, squawking, leaving me and the cafeteria staff to clean up the lunchroom.

My head continues to itch under my hairnet, and when I later go into the bathroom and glance in the mirror, I will realize I looked like Mel from *Alice* all day.

Hugh Jackman
Sweated on Me

I have never been this close at the theatre. Never seen the actual faces of famous people this close. Usually, our town gets the under-under-under-studies in the big musicals when they finally hit town:

Jamie Farr IS the Phantom!

But I have just realized I've been going to these productions three years *after* they've become hits. Kitsy has given me season tickets and restaurant passes to the Frontline Theatre and its City Grill. Her note to me said, "Thought you might like someone else to actually serve your food this time around!"

Frontline is the Broadway theatre of our city, where I get to see the top-of-the-line actors in the touring productions. I have never seen Nathan Lane's face this close. I never knew Patti LuPone was this gorgeous. I can't believe Hugh Jackman is so hot.

When Gary and I start to leave after our very first show at the theatre, we are stopped and asked if we would like to come backstage to meet the cast. They think we are VIPs.

It is an amazing night. But as soon as I get home I am reminded immediately that those aren't our five-thousand-dollar seats, that we are really nobodies in our city's VIP world. Kitsy has left a message. She wants to meet early to discuss our Valentine's Day initiative, which it seems I will fuck up badly without her assistance.

Wade Gets a Girl Friend

Sometimes Kitsy wears a pink baseball cap with a Polo horse on it, her hair pulled into a tiny ponytail that pops through the opening in the back. She says it's because she wants to look "sporty," but I know better. Kitsy has taught me well. She has just had her roots done and doesn't want anyone to think anything has happened to her hair. It's a great trick.

I have never had an adult woman, especially a rich woman, a pretty woman, no less, as a friend. I have spent my life trying to keep women at a distance, so I have never had the chance to get close with them. This is why Kitsy is the first woman to teach me fun little style secrets like:

- It's perfectly acceptable to begin fake-tanning in February, especially since I don't annually take exotic spring vacations. This way, everyone will think I did go on holiday. In addition, I can keep tanning from this point on through winter, because, now, I must, *simply must,* mind you, extend this tan.

- One should always arrive to parties just a little late, so everyone can see your entrance.

- Even though you should constantly get your hair cut and colored, it should never look as though it's just been cut and colored.

• And I am a "summer." I can wear beach sky blues and gecko greens.

Kitsy shares these secrets with me over coffee this morning, following a pattern of recent months, like I've earned an honored place next to her at Tate's lunch table, like we're childhood friends, debutantes separated at birth. But we're not.

Instead, we have been meeting more often in person because I have been asked to formally nominate Kitsy as a candidate for "Woman of Merit," for her donation to Tate and her efforts on its behalf, as well as her volunteer work for countless other organizations. The Woman of Merit is a high honor in our city, bestowed only on the richest, most powerful ladies in town. So I personally fill out Kitsy's nomination form and write her entry letter, as well as a tour de force bio of her life that makes Kitsy sound like Mother Teresa, if the sainted nun had worn pink Lilly Pulitzer habits, had her eyebrows shaped, did her lips in a three-step process, and preferred shopping for $400 pairs of heels instead of cleaning the feet of lepers.

Kitsy tells me about her life in elaborate detail, like she's an aging First Lady describing her life to a famed biographer. She constantly asks, "Are you getting all of this? It's great stuff. You're getting this, right?"

What I'm getting is that she was born into privilege, raised like a privileged child, married a privileged man, had a privileged daughter, and leads a life of privilege. She knows no other life. She leads the life she believes she is supposed to be leading. Volunteer work—rather, the concept of volunteer work—consumes her time. She talks excitedly about this "work," but it all sounds canned and sad. And I believe that Kitsy actually realizes this in the halting moments when she has clarity. Yet this clarity fades quickly, like the gloss she puts on her lips after every sip of coffee; she has been separated from real life too long. The realities of the world are not her problem.

No matter how much caffeine I ingest, I grow bored hearing about her work for the community—I mean, I love the Opera Society, but does it really change the lives of the less fortunate?—and stare at her Land Rover shimmering in the sun. LulaBelle has her paws on the wheel, her little glittery pink nails reflecting the light, and it looks as if she's about to throttle the SUV through the front window of the coffeehouse. I wish the damn dog would.

When Kitsy notices I am beginning to lose interest, she starts giving me more friendly hints about style, or vacation spots, or the newest, hippest restaurant, and, suddenly, her hints soften her stories and work demands, make them seem more like casual requests, from one friend to another.

I know that I have Gary, who has helped reshape, retool, and restyle me, like a midwestern Henry Higgins. He was the first person to tell me that red makes me look like an alcoholic. "And I should know," he said. He was the first to take me to a stylist, not a barber. He was the first to get me out of baggy clothes and into the latest styles. And I know that, despite all of this, Gary was the first person to love me for who I am. Without all of this "help."

So why do I desire it so much? Kitsy sips her two-thousand-calorie latte, and I have huge pangs of guilt. Perhaps this pretty, together, successful, nightmare of a woman actually likes me for who I am. I know that, in essence, I work for her, but perhaps, just perhaps, she simply likes me as a friend. Likes me because I am cute. Likes me because I am fun. Likes me for how I look. Likes me in ways that no one ever did before. Which, sadly, seems justifiable in my world.

I have my first pretty female "best friend."

I am Stanford Blatch; Kitsy is my Carrie Bradshaw. I just happen to ignore the fact that she continues to ask me if I'm getting down every last, golden nugget of her life. I just happen to forget that she instructs me to pick out one thousand *individual, different* Valentine's Day cards by next week for her to hand out to the student body. "No student can get the same card, right? That would just be tacky," she explains.

Kitsy will officially only invite me to coffee one more time. And that's because she will need me to do something for her. So much for true friendship.

"Cupid, Draw Back Your Bow, and Let Your Arrow Go . . ."

"There is no way on God's green earth that I am going to wear that thing!"

Lilly stops by a few days before Valentine's, carrying LulaBelle along with a red unitard featuring a white heart over the chest, and a plastic bow and quiver of arrows whose prongs have been replaced with pointy hearts. Lilly tells me that Kitsy wants me to wear it, so I can be "Cupid" and accompany her around campus while she hands out Valentine's cards on behalf of the Parent and Alumni Associations.

The original kernel of this idea—to bring these two groups to the heightened attention of students and faculty—is not bad. The execution, however, has gone strangely awry. This outfit was not even a part of our coffee conversations, most of which focused on Kitsy's personal sacrifices to help the less fortunate—"I once made phone calls on behalf of the Country Club's new poolhouse drive!"—and barista April's inability to discern between "hot" and "very hot"—"Let me guess, April. You've never used 'tepid' in a sentence, correct?"

Lilly holds the unitard in front of me. "Just try it on, 'K?"

"Would you wear this?"

"I haven't been asked to wear it," she says.

Lilly would be a fabulous presidential press secretary.

"I have a master's degree in journalism from Northwestern, Lilly, and years of work experience. I won't wear a red onesie. I mean, this is insanity, right? Please tell me you agree. She wanted me to be Ronald Reagan, for God's sake. I've already taken a bullet . . . pardon the pun. I will not be Cupid."

"Kitsy will not be happy," she says. Lilly sighs, but it's all for dramatic purposes. She always looks like she got fifteen hours of sleep and a facial. I guess that's what it's like to be twenty-two. "I don't know what I'm going to tell her."

Lilly deposits LulaBelle on my desk, like it's a changing table for a baby. The dog takes a seat—directly on my My-Time calendar, her tiny, fluffy white muff perfectly centered on top of my day's Wheel of Life. Suddenly, I like this dog.

Lilly goes deep into her denim Louis Vuitton handbag and pulls out a miniature replica of my outfit.

"What's going on, Lilly?" I ask.

"Kitsy really wanted you and LulaBelle to dress alike. She thought it would be funny, that you could carry her around, kind of like a Valentine's crime fighter and his trusty sidekick. Kitsy thought the kids would just eat it up."

I am staring at Lilly. I am not smiling.

"It wasn't my idea, 'K?" she says.

Her cell starts trilling, and she pulls it out of her bag. "Can you dress the dog?" she whispers, opening her phone. "I need one of you to play along, for my sake. This is Lilly?" she says into the phone. "Oh, hi, Kitsy! I'm with him right now."

"Tell her I'd love to go with her as she hands out the Valentine's Day cards," I whisper back to Lilly, who is shushing me with her free hand, "but wearing *normal* clothes. This was my original idea, anyway. And I picked out a thousand cards, after all."

Lilly walks into the hallway, and LulaBelle cocks her frayed head and stares at me. I hold up a tiny red onesie in front of her, and she lifts her left paw. She's used to this. *I don't want to like you, dog.* I only like big dogs. But she is awfully cute.

"You know, your owner's the real bitch," I whisper into her soft little ear.

LulaBelle barks. We are one.

Dressing LulaBelle is really like dressing a furry Barbie; Gary and I actually have a Barbie, hidden under our bed, which we still take with us on our vacations, dressing her up like a pocket fag hag, taking pictures of her all over the world for our scrapbook and amusement. There's Barbie mourning at Elvis's gravesite at Graceland. There's Barbie sunning in Puerto Vallarta. Look, there's Barbie spreading her plastic legs and showing her shiny goody bag in Amsterdam's Red Light District.

Lilly walks back in just as I'm pulling the miniature quiver filled with tiny arrows over LulaBelle's back.

"Oh, my God! She's soooo cute!" Lilly squeals. "Listen, I told Kitsy the tights were a bit revealing, 'K? That stopped her third-degree."

"Thanks, Lilly," I say. And then I laugh at the complete absurdity of it all.

"Kitsy does like her drama," Lilly says, laughing.

I see this as my opening, so I ask Lilly the questions I've always wanted to ask but have been too afraid to utter.

"So what's it like working for Kitsy?"

Lilly's doe eyes look deeply into mine, searching for my hidden meaning. She's good. "I love working with her, don't you?"

Touché, Lilly.

"Oh, so do I. She's amazing. So professional, so admired in the community, always has the best ideas."

I look at Lilly; she looks at me. It's like a gun duel at the OK Corral—or the 'K Corral, since Lilly is involved. I fire first. I ask the question I want answered.

"So do you think Kitsy likes me? I'm just wondering."

Lilly looks at me like I'm sweet but pathetic, like the chess club nerd who asks the varsity football captain to go to Homecoming with her.

"I mean, likes us," I say trying to cover.

"Sure. As much as she can."

Then her cell phone starts ringing, and she screams, "Ooooh, goody!" and yanks a Blackberry out of her tote. "This is important," she says. "I have to go. I'm part of 'Makeup Alley,' this secret group of girls that works in cosmetics all over the country. They have this amazing underground supply of hard-to-get makeup. This girl from L.A. who works at MAC Cosmetics just alerted me that she has a new pink lipstick color, 'Sashimi Mimi,' that I've been trying to track down for *months*. I want to surprise Kitsy with it. She'll freak. I have to take this, 'K?"

Lilly grabs LulaBelle, who looks like a dog in drag, and click-clacks away in her spike heels. She has said everything I needed to hear. Not about Makeup Alley, though this secret underground of cosmetics addicts intrigues me. No, it was the other thing she said.

"As much as she can."

Kitsy Grapples with the Horror of Apartheid

Our Black History Month speaker is a young black man who survived the horrors of apartheid. He grew up a prisoner in his own homeland, confined with hundreds of thousands of his fellow people in a few square miles, sleeping in a shack with his ten-member family, battling rats that crawled over his body every single night, battling rats for rotting crumbs of food in garbage cans.

Somehow, this young man survived. And got educated. And wrote a best-selling book that brought attention to the plight of his people.

I battle tears during his entire morning lecture, not wanting to show anyone that I might be weak. Students ask a few questions— "How much money did you get paid for your first book? What's the best city you've ever visited?"—but that's about it. Like most kids, our students get that he's done something important, but, for many, the focus is on the result of his fame, not the reason behind it.

I think, *If he can survive his nightmare, what am I complaining about?* I feel like an utterly contemptible human being, a waste on this planet, for bitching about my plight in this world.

After taking photos of our speaker, I wait to talk with him behind a line of faculty who are having him sign copies of his book. Just as it is my turn to meet him, to tell him how much I admired his speech, his courage, his writing, his story, Kitsy appears in front of me, furious that she has missed his presentation.

"No more morning presentations, understood? Nine A.M. is just too early for parents to get through carpool, run to get a coffee, and then get back to campus. I mean, I still haven't even had my morning latte. Maybe he should put that in his next book. Talk about a real nightmare."

I walk away, forgoing my desire to meet this courageous young man, Kitsy's problems suddenly seeming so much more life-threatening than his.

Surprise! (I Think)

Kitsy is having a Botox party.

I, of course, discover this too late, when I stop by her residence—unannounced, right after work—to drop off an invitation for her inspection and subsequent revamp. I expect Clementine to answer the door, but, instead, Kitsy's new best friend, Chachi, greets me.

I don't really know Chachi that well. Except that she is mean. That she has reported me for a "curious interaction" when she saw me helping the little boy by the fence.

It is too hard for me to keep track of Kitsy's "best friends." She has a supporting cast of M²s following her, rotating in and out of her life, interchangeable look-alikes, like the Darrens in *Bewitched*, or the Beckies in *Roseanne*. They all have names that end in "y" or "i," like Muffy, or Chachi, or Piffy. All I know is that if they are someone, anyone, on the society scene, then Kitsy will have them by her side. At least for a short period of time.

Chachi is holding a white, red-spotted cloth to her forehead. When she removes the hand towel, I can see little dots of blood springing forth, almost as if a baby vampire has attacked her forehead. She looks me over pityingly and wags her finger, me following her like LulaBelle, who has just appeared in the foyer. Chachi leads me into an ornately decorated den—which looks like a set you might see on *All My Children*—where a doctor who looks like Ashton Kutcher is holding a needle over Kitsy's face, and Clementine is serving white wine and hors d'oeuvres to the Pink Ice Barbies. Kitsy may have a lot of interchangeable friends, but it is heartwarming for me to know that Chachi and the Pink Ice Barbies are her "BFFs," "Best Friends Forever," which is what the younger Barbies say constantly to one another. I bet, however, that *forever* in their worlds signifies a significantly shorter time period than in mine.

Kitsy skews her eyes in my direction and, just before the needle slides into the middle of her forehead, she says, "If you take a picture, I will dismember you."

Chachi and the Pink Ice Barbies giggle, sip their Chardonnay, and then hold a towel or ice bag to their foreheads. I begin backpedaling, start to lay the invitation down on an antique sidetable that looks like it once belonged to Benjamin Franklin, when Kitsy yells, "STOP!"

And I do.

She jams a white hand towel to her head and marches toward me, smiling evilly, like a baby that's about to flip applesauce into your hair. I hand her the invite.

"I don't want *that*. I want *you*."

The M²s buzz, like bees that have been swatted at with a rolled-up newspaper, and they swarm around me. Kitsy drags me to the chair and pushes me down into it.

"Doctor?" she asks.

Ashton Kutcher walks over and eyes my face disapprovingly. He looks like he's twelve, for God's sake. He looks like he's dressed up for Halloween, and the fake needle he is holding is filled with sugar water. It's not.

"Problem!" he says, before suddenly jamming the needle right between my eyes. The spot where I have a little dent. From looking puzzled and sad all the time. From squinting because I have astigmatism and 20/400 vision.

The doctor shoots me—without my verbal approval—three more times: once on each side of my eyes and once right in the middle of my forehead. My face feels like the M^2s have attacked and stung me all at once.

Kitsy tells me this is a "little bonus," tells me to enjoy my "refresher." "No charge," she says. "Friends do little favors for each other, don't they, Wade? Friends always do favors for one another."

"That's what friends do," Riffie says, the other Pink Ice Barbies nodding in agreement, whispering in unison like Rain Man, "That's what they do. That's what they do."

I am a tad woozy, holding an ice bag to my forehead, when Mitsy appears, with a friend, and stares at my dilemma. "Are you OK?" she asks.

"Uhh, sure," I say.

"You don't look OK," she says. "Here!" She hands me a Tootsie Roll that she has stuffed in her pocket. "That'll make you feel better!"

And it does, until, on my way out, Kitsy tells me the invite I had brought over needs to be completely redone. And reminds me that she, too, will need favors. In the future.

I walk to my Toyota, which looks like the Clampetts' wagon sitting in front of Kitsy's residence, and stare at myself in the car mirror. Instead of looking angry and bewildered, like usual, I look tight. I look frozen. I look surprised, like someone has just told me the biggest secret in the world. I still look surprised an hour later when Gary gets home.

"You look surprised," he says. "What did you do?"

I tell him, though it wasn't the answer he expected. His answer to me is not the one I expect either. "Your mother would be so disappointed in you."

He's right. My mother is the most selfless person I have ever met. She has been a nurse her whole life, before retiring and becoming a hospice worker. Her life has always been about others. She answers her door at home in old nightgowns, or stained scrubs. She has "jowels" that she inherited from her mother—"The Beck Neck" she has named it. When I saw her over a long weekend recently—when I had a short respite from work, from Kitsy—I asked her about having plastic surgery to remove The Beck Neck. Actually, I pushed her about having cosmetic surgery, virtually unable to hide my disgust at her imperfection. "You have the money," I said. "Why wouldn't you. It's . . ." I thankfully stopped before saying "disgusting."

My mother looked at me—not upset, not mad—just disappointedly, kind of the way she looks at her cookies and pie crusts when she overcooks them. "The Beck Neck gives me character. It's part of who I am," she said.

I remember this now, because I hadn't had a reality check in a while, and I needed these words, this moment, to remind me: My mother has more self-worth than all the M²s at Tate, combined. She doesn't care what anyone thinks about her appearance, only her actions. She would do well at Tate, whose philosophy revolves around being "other-centered." But this is too often a joke, I know, just an en vogue term to demonstrate our compassion. Being other-centered actually means thinking about others first. It's simple. But it's so hard.

I am not there, just like many of the parents and students at Tate are not there. And that's why this job is so damn hard for me. I know someone who is, and a lot of people who aren't.

And, to be honest, I still can't decide which side I'd rather be on.

I remember my mother and her words, try to look confused—after washing my face—at my dilemma in the bathroom mirror the evening of my Botox refresher.

But I won't be able to register that emotion on my face for a few more days.

I'm So Not in the Moment

Sometimes, Gary and I have sex very early in the morning, before the alarm clock rings, before our days even begin. At one time in my life, this used to be so intimate, so special, so magical. I felt the joy and passion of these encounters, the just-awoken suddenness and sensuality, the body asleep but coming alive quickly, my mind and spirit totally in these moments. Just the two of us.

But since working at Tate, since working with Kitsy, we have company in bed with us.

Instead of enjoying these moments, my mind immediately shifts into work mode when I first awake. I steel myself for the day, I subconsciously prepare what I will say for each of my meetings. I have been well trained at Tate.

Gary touches me, kisses me.

And what do I do? I count the fence posts that sit just outside our bedroom window. There are exactly ten in my view. I then count the vinyl siding planks of our neighbor's house. There are exactly fifteen complete planks and five half-planks in my view.

My eyes blur counting them—one, two, three, four, five, six, seven, eight, nine, ten posts; one, two, three, four, five half-planks. No matter how hard I concentrate on counting, though, to keep myself in this neighborhood, this house, this bedroom right now, I think of Kitsy, of the mommies, of my meetings, of Doty, of how much I hate my job, hate the lying. And the counting morphs into, "Good morning, Kitsy! You look great in that skirt. Yes, I do have the centerpieces ordered." Or "Yes, the muffins are being warmed in the oven. No, I would never microwave them for your meeting." And I think how absurd my life is.

And then my mind shifts. I hear Gary. I have forgotten that we are having sex.

"I want you . . . I love you," Gary whispers in the early morning.

"Sure, sure," I say quietly, again counting the posts and planks, mentally practicing my speeches for the day, worried that I've ordered banana nut muffins instead of wild blueberry. I mean, who likes banana nut?

The Guy Holding the Duck Is Chicken

I am quacking as I hold a bright yellow duck in front of a giggling Lila. She is three. Tom and Dan, friends of mine and Gary's, adopted her from Russia. They are good parents. They are, in fact, about the best parents I have ever seen in my life.

As I quack, Tom asks me about Tate Academy. About the possibility of Lila going there.

I look at the little girl. She is bright. She is already highly creative. Her parents are smart and supportive. Hell, they can even afford full tuition. This family would be a great asset to the community. They would make our school a better place. They would make a difference in and out of the classroom.

But I look up at Tom and Dan, and I want to spare them the pain, the inevitability of the heartbreak. Mostly, I want to spare Lila the pain. She will never be the little girl with *those* shoes, but I worry she will be the little girl with *those* parents. I want to spare all of them from the possibility of whispers and hatred. I want to spare them from the chance of missed birthday parties and "Oh, my Gods!"

"I'm sorry," I say to Tom a moment later. *"I didn't hear your question."*

Tom just smiles at me. He is smart. Smart enough to know not to ask me the question again.

The Dance of Loneliness

For a few years now, I have watched the introverted little boy with a mop of blond hair and deep blue eyes grow into a sensitive young man with an abundance of artistic talent and a pained expression, his still-blue eyes constantly darting around, like someone is coming to get him.

He is a senior now. He is slightly effeminate. He is me as a teen, except he is thin and a dancer, not fat and an eater. He is quiet and detached, not loud and funny.

It's a lot like watching a different version of myself grow up. It's like raising my own child from behind a two-way mirror.

I have watched him sing, act, and dance in Tate productions, his talent leaping off the stage, like his long, lithe body, which he quickly scrunches into a sad little comma when he is forced to re-join the rest of the world.

I have seen him interact with his classmates in a please-don't-hurt-me, just-let-me-get-through-this-day sort of way, his brilliance on stage dulled by an uncomfortability with everyday life, like a di-amond ring that needs cleaned after years of being rubbed in hand lotion.

Each year, Tate holds a concert to showcase the talents of its students. There are usually only a few students brave enough at Tate to demonstrate a talent that doesn't involve a ball, bat, or stick. There are usually only one or two boys either brave enough or talented enough to participate, too. I watch the blond boy leap and jump and twirl and spin. He is not just talented in a high school sort of way; he has been blessed.

And instead of simply sitting back and enjoying the concert, it is the most difficult one I attend all year.

Because all around, you can see the kids whisper and giggle. I know this is what kids do when somebody, anybody, does something that is deemed different or "weird," but it's more than this, too. After the concert I hear students laugh and whisper, "Did you see his wrists?" or "What a fag!" On campus, I hear them say even more coarse phrases, ones, though decidedly more clever, that are very similar to what I used to hear after performing in plays. The Barbies, on the other hand, are universally congratulated for their mediocre performances, their hideous jazz-pop-electroshock-inspired dance routine to Justin Timberlake's "Rock Your Body."

This annual concert always bubbles up the bizarre but ever-present dichotomy at Tate: This is a school that places a huge emphasis not only on compassion but also on respecting one another's individual differences and uniqueness. I guess it's OK to be unique by playing lacrosse, but not by dancing. I know there are faculty reaching out to this child, helping him, nurturing him, but he seems alone amongst his peers, and they are the ones that count right now in his life.

Ironically, the blond boy looks much the part of a Mean Mommy son, but he doesn't fit the mold of the typical Tate male student. A Mean Mommy son is a lot like a purebred yellow Lab: all rugged and athletic, with coarse blond hair and curiously distant eyes, full of energy, and square-jawed—certainly not super smart, but, oh, so likable. The son of an M^2 will play football—make that must play football—as well as other sports, such as tennis or water polo or lacrosse; unusual, East Coast sports that will qualify him for Ivy League colleges since he won't be able to get in only on his legacy connections and above-average GPA and SAT. He wears what I used to wear in high school but actually looks good in the clothes: bright polos with the collars turned up, funky jeans, Lacoste jackets. He is confident to the point of being arrogant. He is often hurtful to the point of being cruel.

I want the blond boy to stand up and fight for himself against this pack of popularity, to learn from what I went through. But he can't.

I see this boy one afternoon on my way across campus—to meetings, to take photographs—sitting alone in the courtyard, a beautiful, tranquil space that looks like God, instead of a highly-priced landscaping company, has created it just for moments of reflection.

I look at him and smile. For a second, our eyes meet. And I know, and I believe that he knows I know. The eyes on a gay man are different. They are softer and sweeter, eyes that see not just what's in front of them, but what's actually inside. Eyes that expect hurt and rejection and retribution. Eyes that know fear and loneliness and isolation even at a young age.

I have just seen Tate's early decision/early acceptance college matriculation list, sent earlier this week. This boy will be attending an engineering school next fall. Not a drama school, not an art school, not a dance school, not even a liberal arts college. Engineering. It's what is expected of him by his rich, baby boomer parents who only want him to take the safe route, the one they think will ensure his future but that will only devastate it in the long run. I only hope he will not deny his true talents forever.

Still, I know, this often happens at Tate. Kids are pulled by parents from activity after activity at the first sign of failure, at the first inkling this may not be their calling, or, worse, at the first sign someone might get embarrassed by a wrong note or dropped ball or inappropriate laugh. But isn't that what school, what childhood, what education is all about? Failing, learning to cope, and moving on?

Failure here, though, seems unacceptable. Kids must not only succeed at every single thing they attempt, they must succeed in activities that are universally accepted, generically popular.

Everything in private schools must be safe, structured, and conventional. Here, we have even removed most of the concrete and asphalt from the playgrounds, so children won't hurt themselves when they fall. A spongy surface now lines the playgrounds. When you fall—and believe me, I have—there are no more skinned knees. Only safe, spongy bounces.

At Tate, parents do not like their kids to get below a B minus, because it would be devastating to them, to their reputations, to their child's college transcripts. Children who can't make it at Tate are usually counseled to go elsewhere, told "the fit just isn't right." Those who are not the best students get extra credit, or personal tutors, to elevate the grade. When people pay this much money, you see, they expect results, no matter how badly their kids might be performing in chemistry. It is part of a never-ending chain; top-notch universities do the same. I have worked at these as well. It is too damning, too humiliating, to admit that the institution has taken a student that is not up to par, much less turn one out into the world with hard evidence showing that perhaps, just perhaps, only the best and brightest do not go here. What is lost in this whole process, however, is the child, the young adult, who is struggling, who needs help and support and guidance.

I nod at the blond boy as I pass. He ducks his head, his body becoming a comma, and he disappears into his book. He is reading a book about Alvin Ailey, which he covers with his forearms.

My Well Is Empty

Doty still won't talk to me. It's been weeks now. Not a word. I know it's hard for him to stay silent, but he continues to squeeze by me in the hallway, or take a seat at the far end of the conference table during staff meetings, a ghostly silence and chill to match his all-white outfits.

I have not gone to Doty for help on anything for the past few months. It's partly my depression, partly I don't want him to know what I'm going through, but mostly I don't go to him because I don't need his help. I don't need him for anything. If I talked about Kitsy, I am convinced he would only ask me to write a position paper, or have another useless meeting. So I look through him, like the ghost he resembles. He cannot take this. He craves respect. He must be in control. He must be our faux leader in white. He cannot allow me to be the Ghostbuster. Finally, late one afternoon, Doty comes into my office and closes the door.

"You need to think long and hard about why you're here," he says, his voice shaking with fear and anger. He sounds like he's giving the traffic report from a helicopter. "Remember our review? It should be the work that fills your well, not the people. You are not a teacher, or a counselor, you are a staff member, one piece of the overall puzzle. You are here to do a job, not build relationships."

"Doesn't my job hinge on relationships?" I ask him. "Doesn't your job? Isn't that what our jobs are all about? People give money to people, not places. That's what I've always been taught."

Doty glares at me, like he'd just love to slap the shit out of me.

"Ding-dong!" he says, like a male Avon lady. "I think you need to answer the door."

If I answer it, I want to tell him, I will walk right out, trampling over his bloated body, stepping over his fuzzy head, and never turn back. Except maybe to dress his corpse in an outfit that doesn't make him resemble an iceberg.

"And your office is a sty again, Wade," Doty continues. "You are devolving. Quickly."

He stands, menacingly, as menacingly as Doty can, in front of my desk. I look at him closely, intentionally, staring into his eyes, before dramatically and slowly lowering my eyes to his clothes.

"Only *brides* wear white," I say. "And they only make that choice once in their lives for a reason."

Doty gasps and scurries from my office, like a little mouse does when you flick the lights on in the middle of the night.

Katie Couric
Confuses My Mother

I call my mother because I need to hear her voice. I call, hoping her rambling will make me forget. Instead, she cuts to the quick, like the nurse she has always been, suturing my open wound with one stitch.

"Get out of there," my mom says. "Now."

"I can't. I need the job."

"You don't need a job, you need a passion."

Who is this woman, I think. *Deepak Chopra's understudy?*

"You risked your entire world, your entire family, by being honest about who you are. You showed more courage than an army of men. And now you're afraid? Of what exactly? Of whom? Where's that courage?"

I don't know, I want to tell her. But I say, "Help me. Please?"

She gives me an answer, but it's not the one I expect or want.

"We will, Wade. But it's not up to us. It's all up to you. You have to help yourself. You need to move on like a grown-up. So grow up already."

And then my mother goes on to tell me, for the next hour, how Beyoncé and Bjork are actually the same person. "I saw Beyoncé on the *Today* show with Katie Couric. She is really from Finland. She just tans now, yes, yes, tans, sir."

It is the perfect phone conversation with my mother.

A Web of Lies

I have made an error that, in Kitsy's eyes, is on par with kidnapping LulaBelle, shaving her bald and painting her, well, a color that's not pink. Our office has launched a new student section of the Web site that focuses on the activities and achievements of our youngest children. In designing the Web site, we decided to use a font that would appeal to the kids and their parents, as well as prospective families with young children. I have been designing Web sites for a decade, and the new section is cute, appealing and age-appropriate.

Kitsy disagrees. And she lets me know this in a phone call just as I am ready to leave the office, a Kitsy-free day almost under my belt.

"My daughter has just shown me the new Internet section, and I am shocked and rather appalled, Wade."

My heart races. What could be so offensive? Has someone hijacked our site and posted something inappropriate?

"You have used comic sans as the font. That font is only appropriate if you are a clown or happen to own a Chuck E. Cheese. Please change it to Times New Roman. I must run; I have to get to my Bikram yoga class. TTFN!"

Who *is* she? I refuse to do it. I'm the expert. She's just a mother. She's just my lifeline at Tate. And I'm the mommy handler. This is what I do.

I sit shaking at my desk, looking at the adorable new site we've spent months creating.

And then I make a note to change the font to Times New Roman, knowing the site will undergo a visual transformation that will make it look like a Web site for an accounting firm and not little children.

I sigh.

At least, I tell myself, she didn't ask me to change it to Courier.

Wade Shares His Emotions
with the Office Gals

I'd rather wear skintight Wranglers and sing "It's Raining Men" at a Texas rodeo. My odds of walking out alive from the rodeo are significantly higher than walking out alive from our annual office retreat, held every March.

This year, our office retreat is at a Junior League–type place, which Kitsy has graciously allowed us to use. This place is a charity of choice for the Mean Mommies. In the course of a single morning, they get to go from gossiping over low-fat muffins at Tate to gossiping over lunch at the Country Club to, finally, gossiping over iced tea and lemonade and uneaten homemade cinnamon rolls here, a pink-and-white gingham refuge from the terrazzo floors of Tate or the dark wood of the Country Club.

My twelve female coworkers and I hunker down for the day with Doty in a conference room that looks like it's been decorated by a six-year-old girl with an unlimited credit card.

The morning, of course, starts with doughnuts and drama over the dysfunctional dessert table.

"Aren't you going to have a doughnut?"

This is a fellow staff member. She is scared of gay people. She has told me so. She epitomizes everything I hate about this area; she personally shines the buckle of the Bible Belt. This is the woman who once miraculously managed to slide two gigantic doughnuts around her chubby wrists like food-bracelets just so she could eat them off while singing "Band of Gold." She is a big girl who loves her free food and cannot understand why everyone doesn't feel the same way. Luckily, she is in an office where most people do.

"Nah, I'm fine," I say.

"You need a doughnut. You're too thin. I like a man with some meat on his bones."

I don't, I want to say. "Really, I'm fine."

"Here!"

She holds out a doughnut and actually tries to force-feed it to me, like a tired mother pressing her infant to take some Gerber's, or her boob.

"I don't want it!" I say, like a baby who can suddenly speak.

"Yes . . . you . . . do!"

She misses my mouth and instead presses the doughnut onto the side of my face, which pisses me off. I never lose my temper, in any situation, but the pressure of spending a day with this *Wife Swap* reject is too much. Angry, I grab her hand that is holding the doughnut, like a deranged man force her to smash up the food in her own fist until we are both covered in goop.

"There. Are you happy?" I ask.

"Why are you so angry? It's just a doughnut."

I want to tell her—and the other women stuffing their faces—that I have had my share of doughnuts in my life. I used to secretly buy boxes of Dunkin' Donuts (either the holes or the long johns) and Krispy Kremes (the glazed, and *only* when the sign said "Hot!"), and eat a lucky dozen in my car as I listened over and over to "Total Eclipse of the Heart" on the cheap eighties CD I ordered late one night long ago when I was drunk and lonely.

Doughnuts make me feel miserable now, both mentally and

physically; they transport me to a place I spent three decades trying to escape. Today, I'm a health nut. I don't eat fried dough. I do not do doughnuts. They are one of the dragons I was able to slay in my personal life. I want to be in control of something, anything, in my professional life, and I choose this, since I can't talk about my life at work, or stand up for myself at work.

Doty tries to end the tension by giving me a kolache, which is fried dough stuffed with eggs and bacon. Not really a healthy alternative.

"Here," he says softly, trying to make peace with me. "It's not a doughnut."

I take it, distract everyone by asking what will be for lunch, and then fork up my kolache and place it in my napkin. I remember when I did this once at a local conference and retreat with Cookie Henderson.

"Nice sleight of hand, Houdini," she said to me. "Retreats are like the fat camps I was sent to when I was little, except with more anger and without any counselors."

"I have a little surprise for everyone," Doty announces. He is not wearing white slacks today; he is wearing his version of "office casual," which seems to be garden clogs, sweat pants, and a yellow turtleneck that makes him look jaundiced. I must have missed this look in the last issue of *In Style*. "We are going to pair with a colleague and share something personal with one another, things we don't know about each other. This will build trust and camaraderie."

I, of course, am paired with the gay-hating doughnut girl. Doty gives me an evil wink when he announces this, hoping, I know, that it will end with a big bear hug and not a doughnut fight. He also secretly does it, I know, for revenge.

Doty is firmly in control. And lookin' good.

We head for a pink gingham corner of the room, where I feel I should either be given a mug of hot chocolate and a teddy bear, or a time-out.

Doughnut girl starts our sharing. With a vengeance. She tells me, point blank, that my ongoing anger is because I'm lonely, that I need someone in my life.

"I actually heard that you might be 'funny,' you know . . . 'ho-mo-sex-u-al.' But I've never seen you dress like a lady, so I know that can't be true."

How can we be one of the nation's leading independent schools and still manage to hire people and accept families who are so narrow-minded? How is this humanly possible? These thoughts quickly disappear, however, as she segues into a love connection.

"Soooo, what I'm going to do is set you up with my daughter. She's just like you. She loves the *fine* arts, too. She's always going to yard sales. And she knits doilies and little cat Koozies and has booths at all the local crafts fairs. Big sellers, let me tell you."

She yanks her wallet out of her purse and materializes a photo of her daughter who I mistakenly think at first is LulaBelle. She is pale white—nearly translucent—with matching bleached hair in a spiral perm that cascades into her eyes. She has a pug nose and an underbite. I assume she has eight teats.

"She's something, isn't she?"

"Some thing," I say, separating the words for my own amusement.

She looks at me closely, and I realize that although she loves her daughter she is not proud of her, doesn't believe a word that she's just said.

I used to tell myself that I intentionally—with clear and considerate forethought—chose to work at nonprofit organizations because I needed to believe in a higher cause with my work. It sounds noble, but it is a lie.

In truth, nonprofits have an uncanny ability to draw highly

driven, highly motivated, yet highly flawed people, such as me, such as doughnut girl, such as Doty, those with an utter lack of self-confidence and self-worth—in their bodies and capabilities—and a belief that we do not and will never deserve to work for huge corporations and demand huge salaries and expense accounts, although we do the same quality and level of work.

I used to tell myself that I worked for nonprofits because they would be more accepting to diversity. But men and women in middle America do not get what it's like to work with a gay man, are not even aware that such a thing exists. Most people here feel all men are alike, that I am like every other suburban husband, although I highlight my hair, wear shoes that aren't tasseled loafers, and love to sport trendy chokers. I have a six-pack stomach; I don't down a six-pack every night. And I don't eat meat and potatoes, I don't like NASCAR, I don't enjoy soupin' up my car, and I don't play softball with the fellas.

I also don't have the energy to share any of this with this woman. So I give her my phone number, just to shut her up and stop any possible inquisition, and she spends the rest of the time showing me pictures of her daughter's "art."

"She's a regular Monet," I say.

"Is that a wine?" she asks.

At the end of our retreat day, I am exhausted from the lying, the dating pool, and the food fights. Outside, after everyone has left, as I am about to jump in my car, two staff members walk over to me. I consider them to be friends. "We were paired together today," one says, nervously fingering her necklace, "and we spent our time talking about you."

They both are smiling kindly at me, like I'm wearing a robe and paper slippers and they're talking to me through a barred window at an asylum. She continues, saying, "Wade, work shouldn't be torture.

It should be a joy. You're still a young man. Go find your passion. It's not here, Wade. And it's never going to be. We're telling you this because we love you, and we want you to be happy."

This is exactly what my mother has told me. This is exactly what Gary has told me.

My cell phone rings. I answer too quickly. It's doughnut girl. "I spoke with my daughter. You can call her anytime."

You Have Mail!

This is the incoherent e-mail subject line that I receive from Doty and his assistant, doughnut girl:

    tO Do LIst 4 Wade

The incoherent subject line evolves into an incoherent list, which goes on to remind me of the things I already know I need to do but am reminded of because Doty thinks I'm a disorganized buffoon.

In short, the e-mail pisses me off, not only because of what it says and infers but also because of how it's written. And I'm considered a "passable" writer?

I dash off an assinine message, meaning to forward it to Cookie, but I instead hit "Reply All" and it is sent in-house. I try to unsend it, but it is too late; the history tool on e-mail shows they have already opened and read it.

My message reads:

    What is this? A ransom note? I have a couple of items to add:

    1) KiSS mY aSs
    2) ProOf yoUR E-MaiLS B 4 U sEnd tHeM

3) CuT tHat taLOn U cALL a Nail, dOnUT GirL, SO iT
   woN't HiT tHE CaPS LoCk BuTTon eVerY tiME U ReaCh
   4 tHe "ShiFT" KeY

Thankfully, neither Doty nor doughnut girl has a sense of humor; they are in fact humorless to the point of being sour, like walking lemons, so they both respond with similar e-mails saying my keyboard must be sticking.

Checkmate

Kitsy is writing a check for her new Land Rover. The check is tiny and blue; the Land Rover is big and black.

She had already picked out her new SUV, of course, without me in attendance, but "just for fun" and since her husband is out of town on business for two weeks, she stops in while we're running an errand together and simply trades in this year's model for next year's model. In my eyes, they look the same, but one is new, you see, so they are very different.

We were supposed to be sampling the new key lime petits fours at Gourmet-in-a-Go for an early spring luncheon Kitsy is throwing next week, but she decides getting the car will be more fun. And she's right.

At the Land Rover dealership, Kitsy simply pulls an Edward Jones checkbook out of her Louis Vuitton carryall and writes a check, like she's buying groceries.

Come to think of it, the largest check I have ever written *was* for my groceries. Kitsy doesn't show me the check, of course. That would be tacky. But she does tell me the amount, which I guess isn't considered tacky. The amount is for a "healthy" five figures.

"See you next year!" she tells the salesman, who looks like George Hamilton. All the Land Rover salesmen look like George Hamilton;

all the salesmen at the used car lot where I got my Toyota Corolla looked like Gilbert Gottfried. She pulls out of the lot, her manicured hand waving, as though she's the Rose Bowl queen on a grand float.

"TTFN!" she yells.

This is an out-of-body experience for me, especially considering how my family spends—or refuses to spend—money.

My family still clings to its Depression-era roots. When my Grandma Rouse was alive, she collected tinfoil like it was gold— stealing stray scraps from my parents and then molding and remolding the Reynolds Wrap into tiny squares before unfolding them to use and reuse. She did it until the tinfoil actually disintegrated, like sand in her hands, and even then she would try to piece enough together to cover a casserole, the tinny scraps falling into the food and becoming just another mystery item in the conglomeration. "The next war might be right around the corner," she'd tell us when we'd look at her like she was nuts.

In every restaurant, my Grandma Rouse would immediately sit down and dump all the packets of ketchup, mustard, jelly, and sugar sitting on the table into her purse, politely asking the waitress, "Someone seems to have removed all of our condiments. Could we get refills?" Which she would again dump into her purse.

"This is insanity!" my mother would say over breakfast at our cabin on Sugar Creek, as she opened her eighth tiny packet of grape Knott's Berry Farm jelly that provided barely enough jam to cover the very tip of her knife. "Ted—WHAT!?—toss me another baby jelly."

She was no better, though. While "Choosy Mothers Choose Jif," she often chose the generic brand at Wal-Mart called simply, I think, "Peanut Product," which featured a black-and-white label with a crudely xeroxed peanut lying flat on its back, like it had been shot down and killed in a gun duel with Mr. Peanut. "It tastes just the same," my mother said reassuringly, both of us knowing we would have to stir back in the heavy oil that constantly floated to the top, making it look as if the S.S. *Valdez* had sunk in the jar.

My mother, however, was Imelda Marcos compared to my father, who refused to buy anything new—ever. He bought used cars and mowers and trash compactors, used dishwashers and fireplace inserts. He simply refused to buy clothes. He wore the same things he'd worn in high school and college, no matter how much his body defied the fabric. "You look like Pat Boone," my mother would say to him when he'd come out dressed for a wedding in an argyle sweater and penny loafers.

My family's solution to handling money was and still is simply never to spend it—on anything. The Rouses drove our Rambler until the floorboards rusted away, until I could literally stick my foot through the bottom like Fred Flintstone. I wore patchwork plaid pants and matching vests that my grandmothers made from scraps. I looked like a fat, gay hobo, except I couldn't go ahead and buy a stick to tie my belongings to.

Kitsy's ostentatious display is overwhelming for me. It always is at Tate, no matter how many times a week I witness such overwhelming displays of wealth.

I know that replacing a new car with a new car is just not right. Not necessary.

But still I'm jealous.

Because it sure is a sweet ride.

And Kitsy even lets me drive it in the parking lot of Gourmet-in-a-Go.

"Wheee!" I yell, like a kid riding his new bike. "Wheee!"

She is smiling. But it's not because she's happy for me. No, Kitsy has me exactly where she wants me. She's the one who's really in the driver's seat. And she's known it all along.

Call Waiting

"It's for you."

It's 9:30 P.M. I know who is calling before I even answer. It's work. I know the drill. I can tell by the tone of Gary's voice.

Gary doesn't even hand me the phone anymore; he simply drops it and lets it twirl in a wild circle before it slams into the wall a few times. When people from work have to call me at home, they do not even acknowledge Gary. He is like Casper. Except he's becoming a very unfriendly ghost.

Gary is immune to so many things in his life, but not this. Not this complete lack of acknowledgment. Not this "You don't exist in my world." My heart breaks every time the phone rings in the evening, kind of the way people get scared when the phone rings in the middle of the night: You don't even want to answer.

I take the call. Kitsy needs something, or someone at the school needs something. Somebody needs something. Somebody always needs something. There is a problem. There is always a problem. Something either the caller can't or won't deal with. And so I do. Instead of dealing with the real issues in my life. The phone forever twirling in a circle, forever banging into the wall. Someone on the other end, waiting, waiting, waiting for me.

Just like Gary.

Except he's infinitely more patient.

Spouses Welcome

Gary is losing his patience. He got the mail today, and I have received an invitation to attend a pre–spring break party for school administrators. The invite subtly relays, as it usually does, that spouses are welcome.

Not "partners" or even "significant others."

"Don't go," Gary says. "It's ridiculous. They think you're the only single man on the administration? At your age? Are you telling me they don't know? Are you telling me this isn't intentional?"

I don't know. I do know that I don't want to go. I never want to go. But I do.

And I have to laugh inside, because it's just like sending Anita Bryant to the Castro Street Fair.

Just One for Dinner, Sir?

A few times a year, Tate's administration is invited to the Headmistress's residence for intimate get-togethers. The dinner parties are a way to build camaraderie as well as say "Thank you" for all our hard work.

These parties are akin to torture to me. During the time I have worked at Tate, the Headmistress as well as other administrators have probably called my house after work hours well over one hundred times, especially when there is a crisis on campus or a pending lawsuit. At least half the time, Gary has answered the phone. Yet, he is never acknowledged, never engaged in conversation, never once asked his name.

And I won't be asked either, by anyone, at these get-togethers, where I am forced to engage in conversation for hours. Everyone is surrounded by the ones they love, and here I stand alone, again, although every one of these people has spoken to Gary at one time or another.

Still, I try to make the most of the evening. I typically spend most of these parties making small talk about how wonderfully groundbreaking each of the fifty *CSI*s are, or nodding in agreement about how blasphemous *The Da Vinci Code* is.

I do, however, after two glasses of red wine, typically recommend to a few of the most conservative couples in attendance that *Chuck and Buck* or *Blue Velvet* would make a great little movie rental for their "date nights."

And then I will quietly slip out—after dessert but before coffee—saying I am tired. I wonder, as I drive home, how long it will take the questions about my life, about Gary, to surface now that I am gone.

Talk about your Courageous Conversations.

Mr. Butter Goes on Vacation

"This is so Antonio Banderas–Melanie Griffith, isn't it?"

For my birthday and as a much-needed getaway from work, Gary has surprised me with a trip to an all-inclusive resort in the Caribbean. Tate gets a two-week spring break, just like colleges. This differs little from our two-week holiday break, except now our families can spend a week going to a remote destination like this and the second week "officially" reopening their summer homes in Door County, Wisconsin, or the Upper Peninsula of Michigan, which they typically close after spending Christmas there.

Most of the Academy—faculty, students, parents—disappear, only to return two weeks later tanned and rested. Staff members, on the other hand, are given only two days of vacation during these two weeks.

After years of griping about not getting a real break, Gary offers me one, sweeping me away to a resort with grass huts and beach bars and wandering masseuses, all on white sands that are licked by turquoise waters.

Gary and I are collapsed on two beach chairs near the water. The sun is sparkling, my tropical daiquiri is cool and strong, and it all feels just too perfect, too relaxing.

"This is so Antonio Banderas-Melanie Griffith, isn't it?" I say again to Gary.

I begin to drift off when I hear her voice. The question-command.

I jerk upright and point, like one of my Grampa's Bluetick coon-dogs. I follow the voice and there, pink bikini top undone, white helmet of hair defying the water and wind, is Kitsy.

This can't be happening. I am dreaming, right?

I shake Gary. "Kitsy's here. How the fuck can Kitsy be here, at the same fucking resort we are fucking at?"

Gary looks at me sadly, sweetly, the unthinkable dawning on him. "I heard you mention that people from Tate had gone here last year and loved it," he says. "I never would have dreamed anyone from there would go to the same place twice, much less two years in a row. Oh, my God, I'm sooo sorry."

I have two options. I can avoid Kitsy completely—ducking, running, and hiding every time I hear her voice, hunkering behind bars and buffets, jumping into the surf, masterfully angling beach umbrellas every time I think she might be near, like I'm in a gay witness protection program. Or I can bite the bullet and walk over to say hi.

I reluctantly choose option number two. I chug my daiquiri and walk over to Kitsy.

She is alone now, lying facedown on a towel featuring a giant pink flamingo, reading, of all things, *The Devil Wears Prada.* I stare at her naked back for a moment, her pink, flowered bikini top untied, yet sticking miraculously to her miniscule breasts. I am shocked at how thin she looks unclothed, how she doesn't have a tan line. I think ever so briefly but seriously about pouring a drink down her back, or slapping her ass and running away—like a kid pulling a prank—but instead I gently say, "Kitsy? Hi! Is that you?"

She crooks her head, looks up and stares at me, like an alien has descended before her.

"*Señor Mantequilla?* What are *you* doing *here?*"

Mr. Butter is on vacation, I want to say. *You're supposed to be two thousand miles away. The real question is: What are* you *doing* here?

"I'm on vacation. I actually heard you talk about this place and know that you always have the best taste. So, how long are you staying?"

She looks me up and down, eyeing my very cute but very tight blue-and-brown Sauvage swimsuit. She stops to ogle my crotch, eyeing the bulge disapprovingly, kind of the way she reviews an invitation or centerpiece before ordering me to change it. In my haste to get this moment over with, I forgot to cover up. I feel naked before her—physically and emotionally.

"I'm here a week," she says, still staring at my crotch, but now leaning up just enough for me to see the side of one of her baby boobies. I feel my leg to make sure I haven't turned into a pillar of salt. "I came with a friend. A girls' week away from all the chaos. I deserve it, though, right, with everything I do for you?"

I nod. *Everything you do, right.*

"And then I'm off to finish opening our family cottage for the summer. That's where Mitsy and Mr. Ludington are right now. Two weeks just isn't enough time to get everything done."

I nod.

She stands, pressing her bikini top against her. "Do you mind tying me?" she asks.

This can't be happening. "No. It would be my pleasure," I say.

I tie her top, and she stretches like a cat in the direction of the sun. She leans down, picks up a pink sarong decorated with flowers and hearts, flicks it dramatically like a cape to incite a gay bull, and ties it around her waist.

She is staring at something in the distance. And then she says, like she's pulling a gun and firing a bullet into my heart, "Who's that? Are you here with a *friend,* too?"

I follow her perfectly tanned and manicured index finger, which is shooting an invisible bullet directly at Gary. He has taken a giant beach towel and wrapped it around and around his hair, à la Carmen Miranda, until the headpiece is roughly two feet high. He stands and is now posing—like Salma Hayek on the red carpet. He has incredible timing.

Kitsy is watching this whole scene in horror. What I now realize is that she has already seen us. She already knew we were here. What a bitch. I suddenly start to panic, wondering how much she has seen, what she has noticed. Have Gary and I kissed, or held hands, or splashed each other in the water?

"Oh, him? That's my brother," I say. "My parents were supposed to join us, but my dad got called away on business."

All lies. My father is retired and would never choose to spend a week idle on a beach unless he'd been drugged and kidnapped. My mother would be reading excerpts of the latest Patricia Cornwell novel to a stranger. Oh, and my brother is dead. I am an awful human being.

"Oh," she says. "You don't look anything alike. TTFN!"

I look around as she waves. I think she is talking to someone else, telling them good-bye. She isn't. She's dismissing me. On my vacation. After crushing my pride and humanity in less than two minutes.

"*Adios, Señor Mantequilla.* I just have to get through this book. Everyone's raving, but I find it hard to believe anyone could be so outrageous, don't you?"

"Totally," I nod, backing away from her for some reason, like I've mistakenly entered a secret room and woken up a hungry lion; I must back step cautiously to avoid being mauled. Though I've never seen a lion on a beach.

"She's watching us," I tell Gary upon my return. "I think she knows who you are."

"Who cares?" he says. And then, without warning, he kisses me, full on the lips.

For a split second, I am lost in him, in the warmth of this place and this moment. But I can't stop myself, my paranoia, so I look over at Kitsy from behind the sunglasses she bought for me last fall. They were my first gift from her.

"I refuse to go on like this," Gary says. "You should not hate your job. You should not hate the people with whom you work. You should not care what people think. We've been through all of this before, remember, with your parents and your friends? Is this the way you want the rest of your life to be? This is the life you choose?"

Even thousands of miles away from home, in paradise with the person I love more than my own life, I am haunted by what people think. And I am still lying about my life.

I cannot sleep this week in paradise, no matter how hard the ocean waves or warm breeze or tropical birds try to lull me. I still smell her perfume instead of saltwater, I can still hear Kitsy's piercing voice instead of the tropical birdcalls, I still duck down behind beach umbrellas when I spot a hint of pink.

As I lie in the darkness at night, I think about what Gary has said. His words mirror the last words my brother, Todd, ever said to me, which still resound in my head, just like the roar of his motorcycle as he drove away for the last time:

"Why do you care so much about what people think? It's just bullshit, you know. Just be yourself."

Dinner Is ~~Served~~ Poured!

Miggie has invited me over to her home for dinner. She lives in an ancient, sprawling, decaying mansion in a once-chic area of the city close to the school, where people with money and parasols lived at the turn of the century. The area is lined with giant old trees and giant old houses, gays now revitalizing the area—after years of blight—with new boutiques, antiques shops, restaurants, and coffeehouses.

Miggie's house has a green slate roof and a turret and windows that look like Charles Dickens might pop his head out to say hello. It also has peeling paint, falling shutters, and overgrown bushes. It is both charming and scary, like a home that could double both as a haunted house at Halloween and, with a little cleanup, as a Victorian holiday house on a Christmas tour. Though I have been here many times, this is the first time I have officially been invited after hours. It makes me look at the place in an entirely new light.

I ring the bell and am greeted by Miggie's "new assistant." She leads me to a wood-paneled living room, a room I have never visited, with old books on the dusty, shelf-lined walls.

"Look who the cat dragged in!"

I turn toward the voice, coming from a high-backed leather chair in the corner. It's Cookie, holding a highball. It's going to be a long night.

"What are you doing here?"

"Oh, Miggie and I have been friends for years. We're two of the last old broads to remain standing around these parts."

Suddenly, Miggie materializes like a ghost in front of a makeshift bar in the corner. "I'm so glad you came," she says, tying a scarf featuring miniature ship's steering wheels around her neck. "How about a highball? First drink's on the house."

The next six are, too. I don't even know what's in a highball. This all seems way too *What Ever Happened to Baby Jane?* to me.

I take a seat in a cold leather chair next to a drafty window and listen to four hours of scandalous tales from these women about local schools, society matrons, and city VIPs. It's like listening to an *E! True Hollywood Story* if it had been around in the days of Ed Sullivan. I learn about rumored student affairs with teachers, parent affairs with teachers, alumni affairs with teachers, and teacher affairs with teachers. I doubt much of it is true or accurate, but it is entertaining.

Two hours into "dinner," the assistant brings me a half dozen Saltines covered with spray cheese and a tray of Vienna sausages. That should help the room stop spinning, I think.

"You are a punching bag at work, Wade," Cookie says suddenly. "Why do you let yourself be treated that way?"

And now I know. The old broads invited me here to discuss my well-being, not simply for a never-ending happy hour.

"I'm not a punching bag," I lie. "That's what I was hired to do."

"You were hired to handle educational public relations, not be a personal assistant. You were hired to put systems in place for the parents, to provide them with quality outlets and activities, not just bring them muffins."

"I was hired to be a 'mommy handler,' that's what I was told."

"You were probably told that by someone who's not even there anymore. I was hired to be a nursing home whore," Cookie says.

"That's what I was basically told. But I know better. I raise money from old men, and if I manage to get a little rise in their shorts, so be it."

Miggie chortles, shooting a stream of dark liquid out of her mouth.

"But I choose not to cross that line. You don't even have a line. You don't even have an ounce of self-esteem. You let yourself get treated like crap. You serve as the doormat for—what do you call them?—the Mean Mommies, and they wipe their heels all over you. You have covered for more bad people than Nixon's press secretary. You are not cut out to work like that. The stress will kill you one day. Start focusing on all the wonderful people, not the few bad ones."

I start to interject, start to get angry, but Cookie cuts me off again.

"Has anyone ever met your partner?" she asks. "Anyone from work?"

"No."

"Does anyone know he even exists, besides us?"

"Not really. People call our house when there's an emergency, and Gary answers, but no one has ever acknowledged him, never even said 'hello' to him, or asked his name."

"And do you really expect things to change? Do you?"

This is Miggie, and she is leaning unsteadily forward in her chair, swaying just a bit, like the top of a pine tree in a thunderstorm. "Do you?!" she half-yells.

For once, it hits me. I don't expect it to change anymore. I'm just too scared to move on.

"What are you waiting for? Get on with your life, while you can, Wade. Don't be like us; we let a lot of bad people run our lives for way too long. And look at us now."

Miggie wanted this to be a joke, a funny ending to her diatribe, but it comes out sadly and just sits in the room gasping, like an old dog by the fire.

"Tell us something about Gary," Miggie says, changing the subject. "Just one thing, so we can picture him, picture you happy. It's important we picture you happy, because we can't see it at work."

I don't seem happy at work? This shocks me for some reason. I truly thought I was doing a good job of fooling everyone.

Still, I have had enough highballs to be honest, and I answer her original question.

"I love that Gary's aging," I say. "We watched a sad movie the other night, and he started crying. When we first met and he would cry at a movie, the tears ran straight down his face, fast, without stopping. But last night his tears crissed and crossed through the lines on his face, slowly, like the creek that ran next to my childhood cabin. And I thought to myself, 'My God, I love that river. That is my river. And I want to see it grow. I want our love to grow.' "

Miggie is sniffling, and Cookie is crying. Then they look at one another and, like Rockettes, finish their drinks in unison.

"Who wants another?" Cookie asks, trying to break the tension.

Miggie raises a shaking hand.

"No. Not for me. I better get home," I say. "Gary's waiting for me."

I stay put for a moment, watching Cookie pour whiskey into a finger-smudged glass, from high in the air, like a magician. She transfers the liquor to a stainless canister, mixes it with other liquor, and then shakes the drink quickly, like a can of paint in a mixer, not an ounce spilling. She stops and looks up at me. "Doesn't that feel good to say out loud?" she asks.

It does.

I walk out of the house, get in my car, and look back at two old shadows in the window, silhouettes with tipped elbows.

I will remember this image, their words, forever. For once,

someone has spoken the truth to me, tried to help me. These women, it finally hits me, are really my first female friends, not Kitsy. They're the ones giving me something that truly matters: good advice.

It's funny and touching, when I stop to think about it. Out of all the people in the world, God has sent these two old women to be my rocks.

Who are right now, my incredibly cocktailed rocks.

The Invisible Man

My parents visit campus for the very first time in the spring. They are amazed, impressed, overwhelmed, like everyone is who visits this storybook campus, this Harvard snowglobe in the Midwest. But their eyes see only what's on the outside. Like nearly everyone else.

On our walk, the Headmistress approaches us. She is walking alone, not seeming in a particular hurry to get anywhere fast. But when she sees us, sees me, she picks up her pace, walks swiftly by us, by me, eyes to the ground, without lifting them to greet us.

I know for a fact that it's impossible for her to have missed my parents, considering my mother is wearing a purple frock that looks like it was designed by Bob Mackey's diabolical, designed-challenged twin, and my father is wearing a woman's running suit and Gloria Vanderbilt sunglasses.

Perhaps she is preoccupied or running late for a meeting. Yet the woman who personally greets every child, every parent, every visitor, every stranger on this campus does not greet me, greet my family. The woman who has spoken with Gary hundreds of times on the phone, sought my advice in the middle of dire emergencies, does not even acknowledge the people I love most in this world.

"Who was that?" my mother asks.

"No one," I answer. "Absolutely no one."

Hey, Hey, It's May Day!

I meet Kitsy early one May morning at the coffeehouse, where April is waiting to make me a triple grande, no fat, no whip, white mocha, and Kitsy a vanilla latte with whole milk, whipped cream, and, perhaps, a loogie, all of which are briskly stirred into the drink.

It is a sunny, windy spring day, with big, puffy, white clouds zipping across the blue sky like cotton tumbleweeds. I watch them through the window and wish I were floating away—anywhere—too. It is May Day, and next to football and our holiday concert, May Day is probably the most beloved alumni tradition at Tate.

For Tate women—mothers, daughters, and alumnae—I firmly believe their own May Days run only behind their wedding days as the most memorable event in their lives.

May Day, however, runs last in my book.

May Day has been a part of Tate's long history from the school's inception. It has survived wars and depressions, women's rights and marches for equality, to grow even stronger in the tradition of Tate.

Once a year, for an afternoon, Tate stages this bizarre amalgam of a medieval virginal sacrifice and the Miss America pageant. What started as a simple celebration of spring—little girls in flowered dresses dancing for their parents—is now one of the most lavish, ornate May Day celebrations in the nation, a celebration so grand and elaborate, a spectacle so beautiful and horrific that it has been captured in documentaries and books, and covered by high-society magazines. In this city, it is like the Oscars, each girl's dress, hair, and makeup carefully orchestrated in order to avoid critique by the hundreds of parents, students, alumni, friends, media, and spectators who crowd into the stands and surrounding field for the spectacle. Girls actually begin looking for their dresses years in advance of their senior year May Day, ensuring that they will have a dress that is unique and unrivaled. They spend all day lavishly preparing themselves for the ceremony.

Spectators are careful not to give the ceremony too close an inspection, otherwise they just might see young virginal girls wearing white dancing around a giant, phallic pole—wrapping it, touching it—at an institution that publicly celebrates the mind over the body. *Right?*

While the theme for May Day changes from year to year, the program never alters: The littlest girls, always adorable, kick off May Day, skipping in from behind green hedges to dance for a few moments. They are followed by the eighth-graders, who perform for nearly five minutes. The junior girls carry the traditional dandelion chain onto the May Field, using it like a flowered rope in their dance, before laying it down in a large circle, as if creating an upscale rodeo ring, to frame the senior girls' May Pole dance. The seniors then intricately wrap the May Pole with spring-colored ribbons, which flutter in the wind, followed by their individual bows in front of the crowd and, ultimately, the crowning of the May Queen, the girl who is supposed to represent the best qualities of the senior class.

The theme for this year's May Day is "Singin' in the Rain," and Kitsy wants to ensure that her gift bouquets will match it perfectly. Make that, ensure that her *and her friends'* gift bouquets will match the theme perfectly. Before I can turn the table over, or hide in the men's room, or jump through the front window, Chachi and the Pink Ice Barbies swarm into the coffeehouse and pull up a table and chairs next to me and Kitsy. While seated, Riffie shouts everyone's orders to April. "Put it on my tab!"

Tab? I didn't know you could have a tab here, and, considering her expression, neither did April. This all seems very 1950s, very Doris-Day-and-Audrey-Hepburn-run-into-the-Brown-Derby-and-put-their-Cobb-salads-on-their-tabs.

Once everyone gets their drinks—which are *supposed* to be no-fat, sugar-free vanilla lattes—they simultaneously sip, reapply lipstick, and shout orders, like robotic CoverGirl models, while I scribble flower names and bouquet arrangements and appropriate color combinations.

"What about Lilly?" I ask Kitsy, my fingers cramping. "Can't she help with any of this? I should be busy taking photos. I don't think this really falls under my job description."

Kitsy stares me down with those eyes.

"Lilly is *also* securing blooms, Wade. We need two May Day helpers. This is about tradition. This is about something more than just securing flowers for me. My friends all need assistance, too."

Chachi looks at me and says, "We don't have time to do all the running around, right, girls?"

The M²s giggle and agree, yanking down their java sleeves—for the twentieth time—to ensure by the checkmarks in the appropriate boxes on their cups that their drinks actually match what they ordered.

Ummm, they don't, ladies.

I nod at Kitsy, on the verge of crying, trying to convince myself this is still just "part of my job," and continue to scribble nonsense. I know it doesn't matter what I write at this point, that I will simply say to the gay florists, "May Day. 'Singin' in the Rain.' Save my ass."

And they will. But not before Kitsy says, "Oh, and make sure we have little faux umbrellas, just like Fred Astaire used, in every bouquet. But not in black—in appropriate colors, like pink."

"Yes, pink! We love pink!" the M²s chant in unison.

Kitsy smiles. Chachi and the Pink Ice Barbies smile. I glance over at April, and she smiles, so I smile. Everyone smiles because everyone is happy.

And, with that, I hold up my cup and tip it in these ladies' direction, acknowledging their horticultural and logistical brilliance, celebrating these great women and their great decision-making skills. They are impressed at my chivalry and thaw, ever so slightly. They all clink my paper cup, take long swigs, and then reapply their lipstick.

I smile again. And so does April.

Flower Power

I am sneezing. My eyes are watery and itching, my nose is running.

My Toyota Corolla is stuffed with fresh flowers: lilies, carnations, zinnias, orchids, tulips, daffodils, baby's breath.

My car looks like a Rose Bowl reject, like the float designers got drunk and decorated the interior of a compact car instead of a flatbed trailer by mistake. If I had a pair of wings, I'd look just like the FTD man. But I'm a wingless fairy who just happens to be doing the guy's job.

Besides printing the program, I have nothing to do with the actual staging and execution of May Day. But, depending on the particular year, I sometimes have a lot to do with the intangibles that make the day so beloved by a select few women, so hassle-free for them.

My task this particular May Day is to pick up and deliver carloads of fresh flowers for the M²s. It is tradition for these Mean Mommies to present elaborate spring bouquets to the senior girls, the M²s of the senior girls, as well as to any of the girls who danced in the ceremony and their M²s. In essence, everybody receives a gift bouquet. From me.

It is not tradition for me to do this. And yet, so far, I have gathered probably a few thousand dollars' worth of flowers from the city's top floral designers. My hard labor really begins, however, when the ceremony ends, as I run from car to mommy, depositing bouquets in their arms at the very last minute for them to present without having to sweat or get soaked or muss their outfits in any way.

I am running now, delivering bouquets from car to Mommy, and back. Or I was running. Kitsy stops me midflight with a raised index finger—like she's halting a runaway train with her magic nail—takes a bouquet from my arms, sniffs it deeply, plucks a white daisy with a tiny yellow center from the arrangement, and tucks it behind my ear. *"Es muy bonita, Señor Mantequilla,"* she laughs.

She points a perfectly manicured index finger toward the bleachers, where I am supposed to deposit a few dozen of these bouquets for her and her friends to hand out to the girls. Only, of course, when they are ready to do so. Later.

I start to ask her a question about placement, but she waves me off. "I don't have time to talk . . . to *you,*" she laughs, in front of her friends. "I'm absolutely swamped, right now, as you can see. Wade is so *funny,* isn't he, girls? *Funny?"*

I get it. We all do.

As I start to turn away, she yells, "Catch!" and tosses me the bouquet she was holding. I manage to grab it with my hands and arms already filled, like a circus juggler who can keep adding bowling pin after bowling pin to his act. *"Oooh, muy bien, Señor Mantequilla!"* she laughs, causing everyone to laugh. At me.

With that, Kitsy picks up a video camera and sashays away. For a second, as I hold an armful of bouquets, I can't distinguish her body from these flowers, her blooming dress from these blooms, but she then walks to my right, directly under the May Pole, which is intricately wrapped in multicolored ribbons.

I look at the colorful May Pole and wonder if it would fit up her ass. Stylewise, it would. Sizewise, it might be a little sketchy.

It is a windy day. I watch the pole sway in the stiff May breeze.

Kitsy is gabbing and laughing and incorrectly using her video camera, which I know she will blame me for when she gets home and sees that nothing has been recorded, when only black appears on her flatscreen. The May Pole sways dramatically in the wind. *Go down!* I think. *Fall.* I even try to blow a bit harder to nudge the damn thing, but it stays firmly entrenched in the sod.

I close my eyes for a second and pray that the wind will suddenly just knock it over, pinning Kitsy underneath, like a pink-cloaked wicked witch, just her pink shoes sticking out, her feet making a final twitch.

But it doesn't. That only happens in the movies. So I dump the blooms in the spot Kitsy designated with her nail.

I watch Kitsy point and place pretty people in perfect positions; she is the director of her own beautiful documentary.

I walk back to my Corolla and put a big bear hug on four more bouquets, water trickling down the front of my shirt. I look like a queen. Not *the* queen, mind you. Just a queen, hauling flowers for rich women, the wind blowing my hair around, like Dorothy in the tornado. Except I won't even be lucky enough to get knocked out and wake up in a magical new place.

I look over and see Mitsy waving at me. "Are you OK?" she mouths.

I nod my head "no" today.

The little girl runs over to help me, ignoring her mother's protests.

Pomp and Circumstance

Tate's Commencement ceremony is my favorite event of the year. Partly because I envy the graduates, who actually get to leave forever, and partly because the event celebrates the best the school has to offer.

Proud families crowd the campus, faculty dress in their brightly colored robes and hoods, famed and successful alumni return to speak, and students march off to great colleges and universities, eager to conquer the world. And they will: A few decades from now, I know many of these kids, sitting onstage, right here, right now, will be making decisions that could literally change our world.

This scares me a little, but it also—looking at our faculty—gives me hope, that this group will be the one who listened, who got it right, who have been imbued with compassion and tolerance, who will be better parents and better citizens.

I watch today's ceremony, finally realizing life is made up of mini-graduations. We all celebrate the "big ones," the traditions in which most of us partake—high school and college graduations, birthdays, weddings, anniversaries. But we rarely celebrate our little successes, the baby steps we take that make us the people we are today. These are the unheralded moments, the silent celebrations, but the ones that truly matter most in life.

Unlike these great kids, I think I am still waiting to graduate.

I've Fallen and I
Can't Get Up

I am in the middle of coordinating a photo shoot for our new admission materials. It is the end of the year, and our campus is beginning to explode in color, pastel-popping bushes and blooms strobing across Tate's acreage like paparazzi flashbulbs.

To handle the shoot, we have flown in a very hip New York City photographer, who looks like Orlando Bloom, and he has brought along an entourage of hip, pale, pretty people in very tight black T-shirts. I am just handing the day's shoot to them when Kitsy calls me from carpool. "I need you!" she exclaims. "TT—"

"I'm in the middle of a meeting. I can't come right now," I say.

"—FN," she finishes. "I have to talk to you. It's vital."

"Kitsy, I can't right now. We have photographers in from New York, and—"

She doesn't care. I could be having open heart surgery right now and she'd still expect me to come to carpool.

"You will come . . . now!"

She hangs up. Hip people are staring at me. They all have very sad, yet very bemused expressions on their faces, like they can't wait to get out of earshot so they can talk about me. They heard the conversation; they know my life. My sham of a career.

Still, I try to cover, as always, to act cool and unaffected no matter how many times life here slaps me in the face. Yet in my attempt to hang the phone back up while remaining trendy and cool, I trip over a bottom desk drawer I have left open and fall, phone still in hand, backward into my bookcase. In an attempt to steady myself, I ricochet the phone off my crotch and claw at the artwork hanging above my bookshelf. It is a three-dimensional piece of our city's zoo that sixth-graders did in art class. It features a myriad of hand-painted clay animals and gates and trees that have been glued onto a thick backing. As I go down, I claw three penguins off the portrait and knock over my bookshelf, before my left ass cheek bangs into the open drawer. I am whimpering. Softly, yet audibly, like a puppy that's being crate-trained.

The hip people don't move any of their taut, pale muscles in any attempt to help me whatsoever. They just stare. At me. Covered in books and clay penguins. I am very close to crying. This feels just like the time I was eleven and fell skating at the roller rink. It was the first and last skating party to which I was ever invited. I bloodied my chin and ripped the crotch out of my purple polyester pants to "Afternoon Delight." Come to think of it, this also feels eerily similar to when Mrs. Van Cleve "shoved" me down a flight of stairs last fall. And to when I tumbled down the front steps with Kitsy's stolen donations at Christmas. Why am I always on the ground, bleeding and nearly comatose in front of pretty people?

I don't even bother yoga chanting to center myself. I simply try and get up with as much dignity as I can muster—as much as one can when he's yet again fallen like a drunken hooker in stilettos—and start to escort the hip people to their first location, wondering why a girl who looks like Parker Posey keeps staring at my ass. On our way there, my cell phone rings. Caller ID shows it is Kitsy. I don't answer. I simply veer off from the entourage—pointing them in the right direction—and head toward carpool.

"You're exposed," Kitsy says just as I step up and onto the running board of her Land Rover and peer into her SUV though a crack in the passenger window.

"What?"

"You seem to have ripped your pants," she says, smiling. "I could see it all the way from the carpool lane. I'm humiliated for you. And I'm angry at you. You're very late."

I hold onto the top of the window and swivel my head to look at my rear. Yes, I have ripped the ass out of my trousers. And, of course, I don't know it until this moment, Kitsy pointing it out in carpool with her French manicured talon just a second before a cool breeze mocks me by hitting my butt cheek.

Suddenly, to recapture my attention, she punches the gas, throwing me off the car and nearly under her tire. I turn again to look at my ass; I can actually see the bottom part of my butt cheek, which I cover with my hands as if I've just had a towel ripped off me.

"Now, what I wanted to talk to you about was . . ." Kitsy starts.

I watch her lips move, but, this morning, I see only white instead of pink, my ears hear only static instead of her clipped, overenunciated syntax.

For once, I am furious and, for the first time, actually show my temper. Actually tell the truth. Actually unleash every ounce of rage that has been building in me for months, building in me since I was intentionally shoved down a flight of stairs and Kitsy opted not to help me up, since I dressed like Ronald Reagan, since I sold my soul to this woman for clothes and great theatre tickets and a pathetic chance to be liked by one of those popular people who has never liked me. And so I simply pop, like the tinfoil top of a Jiffy Pop popcorn that's been left over a campfire too long. As I speak, I think about stopping myself. Either it's too late, or I don't want to. These concepts simply merge and then vanish as I yell.

"Actually, I fell because of you. I rushed through an important meeting . . . humiliated myself. . . . Do you understand how ludicrous all of this is? Do you? Do you get that this is my career? My life? That I'm wasting my life? That my career is about taking crap from a few bored, rich women? That my life is about muffins and mommies? It's a joke. A complete and utter joke. And do you want to know what's worse? You're a joke, and don't even realize it. You are an absolutely pathetic and contemptible human being . . . and I'm sick of taking your shit."

Kitsy is staring at me. Through me, really. And then, as though a director—Ang Lee, perhaps—has called for it, the sun hits her eyes—her Blue Raspberry Mr. Misty Dairy Queen eyes—and I feel frozen solid, through and through, though it is a very warm morning.

Kitsy is not smiling.

And she won't for a long time.

In fact, she will simply drive away, without saying another word. Only LulaBelle will comment, barking either a "You're so fucked" or "I'll miss you, pal" to me—I can't distinguish—as the Land Rover does a U-y.

But Kitsy will quickly say a lot to a lot of other people, telling Chachi, and the Pink Ice Barbies, and whoever she happens upon exactly why I don't have a ring on my finger. And they will tell two people. And so on. And so on. And so on.

My so-called friendship with Kitsy is over. And it's all because of the one thing neither a gay man nor a rich woman can ever bear: public humiliation.

I turn to go back inside, and as I do, I twist my head as far as it can go to study my butt cheek, which is turning black-and-blue, and red. I am bruised and bleeding, the fabric around my torn pocket turning a deep red.

I fell because I was disorganized.

And then I laugh: It's Doty's perfect revenge.

At least I'm not wearing white, I think, or someone would have already called an ambulance.

Letter Perfect

My pretend friend is gone. She was just a Mean Mommy after all. I was just kidding myself.

The next week, I discover that another "anonymous" letter has been sent to the community. This time the letter is about me, and it informs everyone that I am gay.

How do I know?

I get a copy of the letter at home. Along with my phone bill and a Pottery Barn catalog.

But I'm not really that mad. Shocked, yes. Hurt, yes. Terrified, yes. But mad, not so much. For many reasons. For one, Kitsy didn't tell anyone about my outburst. For another, the letter is one of the first truly honest things this place has ever written. I have already been secretly told yet another letter about someone else is ready to be sent, a new scandal to focus on, another distraction to, hopefully, take the heat off me.

But it's not as though everyone didn't know about me, I finally realize. It's just that someone had the guts to finally say it.

It just wasn't me.

Good to the Last Drop

M iggie leaves a note in my box. It is attached to a small, red canister of Folgers. It basically states:

"Heard about the letter. I don't know of many people who received it. It's already old news anyway. A much belated thank-you for all the crappy coffee. Thought I'd return the favor. You'll need the caffeine one day when you finally have the courage to write about me, about yourself, about all this, when you need to stay up around the clock to get every single memory out."

But I don't have the courage yet to write about any of this. Right now, I don't have the energy to do much of anything. I am too busy inventing a secret crisis communications plan to save myself, since I do not feel protected under Tate's non-discrimination policy, since sexual orientation is not included. This *is* big news to me. I feel all alone. So I go into survival mode.

I use my passable writing talents to secretly draft a public statement that details how a disgruntled former employee simply wanted revenge and wrote an outrageous letter to discredit me and the Academy.

I cannot sink any lower.

I wait and wait to be swept up in a storm of gossip, for Kitsy to strike again, for the snipers to send their next letter, for me to be called into a private meeting with attorneys and told that I am no longer welcome to come back to work here. I wait for days, panicked, my heart racing, but, shockingly, I never have to defend myself, because no one ever says a word to me about the letter. The desire, I now fully realize, to preserve reputation trumps everything. No one here can show weakness. And if they do, we simply make it go away, make it disappear.

Which is exactly what I do. I take my coffee and my letter home and simply shove them away. Like I do every bad memory in my life.

Party Planner

While Kitsy may no longer speak to me, it doesn't mean she still doesn't need my help. She does. She has to finish her year in high style. In control. She has to shove my face into the mud one more time just to flex her muscles, just to show who's stronger, like the mean boys did to me once after school, asking, "Does it taste like chocolate, fat boy?" as my face went into the rain-soaked ground.

So even though Kitsy doesn't speak to me in person, she does speak to me through Lilly, her Mandy Moore–inspired oracle.

It seems Mitsy's birthday falls the first week of June, while Tate is officially still in session. She sends Lilly to me—following a pretty nightmarish year, overall—at a point in which I am physically and emotionally bruised and battered, at a time in which I just want to crawl into a bunker for a little while, take cover and lick my wounds. This isn't an option.

"Kitsy says she needs two favors, 'K? She's way mad at you," Lilly says. "I think it's OK, you know, about you . . . your life, your choice. It's OK with Kitsy, too, I think. She, like, just can't take rejection real well, you know? It's hard for her at home."

It doesn't have to be hard for her, I want to tell Lilly. But I don't. I just listen.

"Kitsy needs you to help me run errands for Mitsy's birthday party. I have the list; she says she can't do it all herself, and she knew that you would be available since, well, you kind of have to be."

Sure, I think, *I can fit in a birthday party for the woman who tried to ruin my life.*

I know my plight of yesterday probably doesn't even register with Kitsy today. So I say nothing. I don't need to speak. Lilly does all the talking.

"Kitsy wants to make it clear that she is *not* inviting Mitsy's whole class to the party. They just wouldn't, you know, fit in, she says. She said you'd look like that, that you wouldn't understand, but she said to tell you that it's just a little birthday party. Mitsy's not friends with everyone. It's impossible to be."

Lilly looks down at her heels, which are really high, and twirls her hair.

"Say it, Lilly. Just tell me. It's OK."

"Kitsy says you owe her. Big. So she needs you to cover me, cover her, in case there are questions about why the whole class wasn't invited. She wants you to say you worked with her on it and there must have been some weird oversight, if you're asked."

Lilly looks again at her pretty shoes, and they somehow give her a burst of energy, a little touch of sunshine, like she just discovered that Banana Republic is out of her size zero jeans, but quickly learns that the Gap isn't.

Bravo, Lilly. So that's how you survive.

"I'm sure it'll be fine. I'm sure there won't be any questions. Why would you help with something like this anyway, right?" she says. "I've gotta go, but I'll be back with the list, 'K?"

On her way out the door, she stops suddenly and turns. "I just wanted to say I'm sorry . . . about everything," she says, her head down, her thick blond hair tumbling in front of her face. "I'm not a bad person. I want you to know that. But I'm trapped, too. My parents are friends with Kitsy, and I can't let them down. I can't fail at this. This is too important to them. I really want to be a fashion designer, but my dad thinks *that* is too frivolous, thinks New York is Sodom and Gomorrah. I don't have any other option. I didn't go to Tate. I need Kitsy's help. I need her connections. She says she's going to help me make it, you know? Help me start my very own business. She has a lot of very important friends."

"I know," I say. "I don't blame you."

She lifts her head and smiles. She looks tired today, not as fresh as she did earlier this year. There are puffy little bags under her big innocent eyes. *Welcome to my world.* She starts to head out, but I stop her.

"Lilly? Watch out for the lions. They'll eat you alive. That sounds completely lame, I know, but someone told me that once, and I thought I'd pass it along."

Lilly takes a deep breath—a cleansing breath—exhales, and attempts to smile. "Thanks," she says, "but I think it's already too late."

And with that, she heads off to meet Kitsy.

Is it too late?

My heart drops to my shoes, which are not as nice as Lilly's. I am back at the same place I always find myself here at Tate. Torn between doing the right thing and the wrong thing. How come I always walk to the dark side?

Though I do not know the invitation list, do not know the kids being omitted from Kitsy's holiday party, I have a pretty good idea from earlier clues.

I open my bottom desk drawer and retrieve a copy of "Tate Talk," our school's parent directory. I turn immediately to Mitsy's class, where I begin scanning the names. My heart stops. The little boy who wrote "I'm sad" in red cups is in Mitsy's class, along with his little friend who wasn't invited to the fall party. *What a strange coincidence!*

I know it's nearly impossible not to have cliques in a school, any school, especially in an institution that too often prides itself on cliques and cronyism and connections. But six-year-olds have cliques? No, I realize, they don't. But their mommies might.

I go to my office door and look out the hallway windows, watching Lilly jump into her red Saab convertible. I realize that I am utterly dispensable. Lilly is dispensible. We are all utterly dispensable, replaceable, in Kisty's world, just like her friends. We're not even her friends. We're her employees. I should go directly to the Headmistress or to Doty and report this. That would be the appropriate thing to do. But I don't. I've never done that and never will. I keep it all to myself. I know now that if I don't lie for Kitsy, she will simply go and have someone else do her dirty work. For once, I realize Kitsy will never change, never embrace the person she could be. There is too much baggage. Too much Louis Vuitton baggage.

I, however, am significantly more unfettered.

I walk back to my office and pick up my Grampa Shipman's old Mason jar filled with pennies, which I keep in my desk. I turn them over and over, watching the old, greening pennies plop from side to side.

These pennies remind me of what a precious gift education is.

My Grampa Shipman—my mother's father—saved pennies, collected change, in a big, old, cracked butter crock. One penny at a time, four or five cents a week, maybe a dime or a quarter tossed in when times were good. By the time my mother went to college, this laborer who never graduated high school had saved just enough money to change the course of his family's lives forever.

With a lot of pennies.

The power of his pennies, the leftover ones I consciously saved and placed in one of his old Mason jars, is my daily reminder.

When I am stressed, I grab the jar off my desk and hold onto it tightly. When I do this, I can still feel my grampa's steely presence, can still hear the plunk of those pennies echoing in the crock in his garage.

The cost of education is truly priceless.

So when did I lose that concept here?

I grab the jar and hold tightly, remembering the past year, the words flooding back from my memory:

"I'm sad!"

"Where did you get those shoes? Oh . . . my . . . God!"

"The lions will eat you alive."

There is really only one decision I can make this time. I keep it all silent, as usual, and decide to play along with Kitsy, and, for once, actually do what I was originally hired to do.

Handle a mommy.

Let's Review the Invitation List, Shall We?

Lilly stops by again later in the day, after everyone has left. She has a laundry list of things for me to do in advance of the party and runs through them chirpily. It's like listening to a cardinal on crack. Lilly is resilient, if nothing else.

"The theme for Mitsy's birthday is is 'Pink Perfection.' Cute, huh? She got the idea from this awesome party planner. Kitsy just loves pink. Here's the list of stuff to get; I thought we could split it up fifty-fifty, 'K?"

The to-do list, of course, is on pink stationery and includes the following details:

INVITE

Pink and ready to go from Papyrus. The invitation will instruct the little girls to wear their finest pink and white fashions; boys are to wear white shirts and khaki shorts; they will get pink boutonnieres when they arrive. Lilly has already calligraphied the names and addresses of Mitsy's invited classmates on the envelopes.

DECORATIONS

Yards and yards of pink tulle, yards and yards of pink ribbon, which will circle the perimeter of the slate patio.

PARTY FAVORS
Summer flip-flops from Gap Kids are to be purchased; they will be jazzed up with bows made from a variety of pink-and-white patterned ribbons.

Pretty pink ribbons and shiny pink beads also need to be purchased from Sew Cool! so girls can string their own jewelry at a special table laden with these items.

Boys will receive pink Lacoste polos.

MENU
The food, of course, will be pink and white, and the menu will include the following items:

A polka dot cake with pink icing and press-on white circles of sugar, made by Sweetie Pie's.
Pink punch (pink sherbet and 7-Up)
Fresh strawberries
Pink-dyed pasta
Strawberry jam sandwiches
Strawberry ice cream

We split up the to-do list. There is only one item I specifically but subtly request this time around.

"I can pick up the invites," I say casually. "If you just want to leave me those envelopes, I can hand-stamp those, too. We have tons of left-over stamps in the office—even ones with those pinky hearts that say 'Love'. I know Kitsy would want everything hand stamped."

"Oh, my God! That's so perfect!" Lilly chirps, handing them over to me. "You are, like, so the best. What a trouper! I gotta go, 'K? We'll chat later. TTFN!"

Just like that, I had a party to plan. And I was excited to get to work on the guest list, especially after scanning the envelopes to realize that I had been correct: two kids had been "inadvertently" left off of it.

Mr. Counterfeiter

In addition to being a good fixer of photographs, I am also a good forger. I have years of experience signing letters for absentee volunteers and executives, rich men and women who are too busy to show up to do their actual volunteer work. Cookie has trained me well. Of course, our office has the ability to scan in volunteers' signatures, but our constituency knows the difference, knows to lick its collective finger and run it across the ink to see if it's real, to see if someone really took the time to thank them for their $10,000 Annual Fund gift.

I can do it all. Sign any name, match any style of writing. I am a first-rate forger. I am the perfect white-, or at Tate, pink-collar criminal.

Later in the day, I pick up the printed pink invitations from Papyrus along with two matching blank invitations and a couple of extra envelopes. I bring everything back to work, where, after everyone is gone, I make color copies of the real invites and gluestick those to the blank ones. I then hand-stamp the envelopes. Finally, I hunt down a matching calligraphy pen and, in my best imitation of Lilly's loopy, girlish writing, add these two final invites to the stack: one for a little boy and one for a little girl. I do a good job; great, in fact. The invites are first-rate knockoffs, and the names on the envelopes match the originals perfectly. I even put little hearts over the *i*'s in the kids' names, instead of dots. Lilly is so Lilly.

And, to ensure I don't get caught—like any criminal worth his salt—I stop at the dumpster of a local apartment complex and throw away the calligraphy pen. I then drive to every family's home and, when I am sure no one is there, personally place the invitations in their mailboxes. This way, they can never be traced, either back to Tate's mailroom, or the post office from where they may have originated. I know that if I am ever asked by someone who saved their envelope and wonders why there is no postmark, or by someone Kitsy sends my way, I will simply say, "I just provided the stamps. Why in the world would I help with a little girl's birthday party anyway?"

Even though I still secretly had to run all over town, filling my car with everything pink, I knew, for once, that I had actually done my job, done what the school would have wanted, actually done what God had sent me here to do: help children.

Everyone in the Pool!
(Take Two)

June 1978. It is my last day of school in seventh grade. Every year since first grade, Josh Matthews has handed out on the last day of school invitations to his big summer birthday party. For years, he has hand-delivered envelopes his mother has personally addressed to the popular kids in our class, who promptly pull out invites in the shape of hot dogs or hamburgers, or circus tents, or baseballs.

Today, in between classes, Josh slides invitations into certain kids' lockers. I sprint to my locker after every class to see if one is waiting. It's not. My best friend, Nicole, however, gets one. It is in the shape of a swimming pool. Josh has gotten an above-ground pool as his birthday gift this year, and he is having a pool party to celebrate.

Though I am not invited, Nicole asks me to go as her "date." I tag along because I, of course, want to be at the popular party, no matter what.

We show up, Nicole wearing a tie-dye bikini and sporting a new Dorothy Hamill wedge that looks like a blond chunk of iceberg lettuce. She, of course, dumps me fifteen minutes into the party to stalk a guy she has a crush on, leaving me alone. I stand by the edge of the pool wearing oversized aqua swim trunks and a giant H.R.

Pufnstuf T-shirt, watching everyone splash and float, staring at the boys confident enough to swim without shirts.

Out of nowhere, a dripping Josh Matthews appears. I stare at his perfection. He looks exactly like Lance Kerwin from my favorite TV show, *James at 15*.

"Ummm, were you invited?" he asks, like he has no idea who I am, like we haven't gone to school together our entire lives.

"Nicole kind of invited me as her date."

I follow Josh's gorgeous eyes in the direction of Nicole, who is giggling and flipping her wedge by the boy she likes.

"I can see," Josh says. "Well, you kind of have to do something to stay."

"Ummm, OK," I say.

"Cool." I follow Josh's perfect torso up the stairs of the pool, where he promptly pushes me into the water. "Dogpile on Wade!" he screams, as he jumps directly onto my back. I am subsequently dunked, pushed, stripped, shoved, and nearly drowned for the next two hours, while Nicole makes out with a boy who looks like Shaun Cassidy.

I go home after the party and beg my mother to buy an above-ground swimming pool. "Puh-leeasse!" I beg. "I need it to make me popular."

She looks at me in her nurse's uniform and tells me what I expected but didn't want to hear. "We have Sugar Creek," she said. "And people shouldn't like you for what you have or what you can do for them, they should like you for who you are. If they don't, they're really not your friends."

Not groundbreaking advice, really, but it is what every parent should say, what every child should hear, in a situation like this.

Ironically, I will be invited to Josh's party the next summer. My envelope will state "Designated Dunkee!" on the outside instead of my name.

I don't attend the summer after I finish junior high. Instead, my brother will be killed in a motorcycle accident. For years, I try and convince myself I wouldn't have attended anyway, that I was tired of being humiliated, tired of going to places and being with people who only wanted me there if I could do something *for* them.

But I never had a chance to prove it to myself.

Until now.

Guess What I Learned
in School Today?

The Monday after Mitsy's birthday party, the last week of school, as I make my way across campus to a meeting, I see the little boy making a sandcastle on the Lower School playground and stop to ask him how his weekend was. Instead of weekend, however, my mouth jumps ahead of my brain and I mistakenly say "party" instead.

"Awesome! Really awesome!" he says, his eyes aglow, sand trickling between his fingers. It is then I notice he is still wearing his pink boutonniere, even though it is now wilted and a bit flattened.

"I'm glad," I say.

His mom is standing a few feet away. I look over and smile. She introduces herself, and I do the same. "How did you know about the party?" she asks.

Must . . . think . . . quickly.

"Oh, I work with Kitsy. She told me a little about it."

The line comes across as rehearsed, kind of like I am on trial for murder and talking with the press for the first time.

The mother smiles at me, like moms do at kids when they've done something sweet and unexpected, like made their bed without being told, or tried to cook French toast on Mother's Day.

"Well, the party was very nice. I was rather surprised to get the invitation," she says. "And Kitsy seemed rather surprised to see us there at first—she actually asked for our invitation and then kept it—but she spent most of the time with her friends. I didn't talk to her, but that doesn't matter. What matters is that the whole class was there. What matters is that Mitsy personally welcomed every guest there. What matters is that I got to know a lot of great moms. It's been . . . hard this year. He's only a little boy. This is new to us; I blame myself a little, too. But this is a positive way to end the year. It gives me hope."

"I'm so glad he was able to go, then," I say. "Kitsy can throw a great party."

"It meant a lot to him," she says, looking at her child. "It meant a lot to me."

I duck my head and take a deep breath. This is like one of those emotional moments in a movie that captures you totally by surprise, where you gag-cry out loud, humiliating yourself in front of the audience. I do this a lot in movies—like when Shirley MacLaine pats the seat next to her at the end of *Terms of Endearment* so her granddaughter will move closer to her; I have to use every ounce of self-control to not let it happen now.

It meant a lot to me, I want to say. But instead, I say, "I have to run to a meeting. It was very nice to meet you."

I walk away, turning back just long enough to see that the mother is watching me, still smiling.

I slow, needing just another moment to regain my composure before entering another meeting as Wade, the hologram.

It is a glorious day on campus, and I breathe in the warmth—that brief moment just before spring quickly turns to summer—to smell the earth coming back to life.

To feel myself coming back to life.

Mail Call

That night, when I get home, I have two pieces of mail.

I know instantly who the first letter is from, because the envelope is pink. Lilly Pulitzer pink, of course.

Written in her note is just a single letter—"K."

I smile, for some reason, and take a seat on my tiny white front porch swing and open the other card, too. It is from Gary. On the cover is a picture of a little blond boy holding the world over his head, like a baby Hercules.

Gary's card contains four words.

"My hero. Love, Gary."

I keep only one of the cards.

Wade Earns His Diploma

In the end, I truly wish there had been a more dramatic event to bring all of this to a conclusion. My fantasy had always been to turn over a table on Doty, or at the coffeehouse in the middle of a meeting with Kitsy.

But no tables turned, no Poles plunged.

Instead, I decided to leave Tate, to flee from Kitsy, to make a change in my life. But I found myself in eerily similar positions at other places, and I wondered how widespread the Mean Mommy dilemma truly was.

Then, ironically, just a few years later, I was asked to return to Tate—like a weathered head coach—for a second chance. And I did.

Why? you gasp.

I still ask myself the same question today. I know, down deep, it was because I was so used to covering up the pain and the past, to always forging ahead, to ignoring little problems—like basements that leaked—to big problems—like staying in the closet for so long and not taking charge of my life. Perhaps I wanted redemption, or revenge, the two mingling into one amorphous lump. Still, I convinced myself into believing that I returned because I needed to make a difference, needed to believe I was bigger than Kitsy. I was told that I was, that the school needed me, that it had changed. And it had. A wonderful administration was in place. Most leadership positions were filled by a great group of women who worked for, and not against, the school. But, like in an old Alfred Hitchcock movie, the old guard still lurked in the shadows, a select few M²s were still fighting their fight. Thankfully, however, not against me this time.

A few years into my second go-round, I was simply helping Gary spring clean our little bungalow. This spring day, the windows were open, a breeze blowing my Grandma's old curtains, and our Swiffer skills were finally being used in a deep and meaningful way.

And that's when, as I cleaned the kitchen, I stumbled across Miggie's canister of Folgers. Sitting forgotten in the back of the kitchen cabinet.

And then Kitsy's letter about me. Sitting at the bottom of a little-used kitchen drawer, buried under chocolate chip cookie recipes and an overstuffed, red Hannah Hansen coupon holder.

I sat in the middle of our eight-by-nine-foot parquet-floored kitchen, hugging the Folgers, reading the letter, remembering that year with Kitsy. Remembering why I wanted to work at Tate in the first place. Remembering why I had returned. Remembering why, once again, I needed to leave. Remembering, for the first time in a long time, exactly who I was, who I wanted to be when I grew up, and why I still wasn't writing.

And that's when the lightbulb finally went off in my head, the phone started ringing in my mind. After years of sleep, I finally received my wake-up call.

And so, instead of cleaning, I started to write, that day, in longhand, sitting spread-eagled in the middle of the kitchen floor. I began to finish the letter that Kitsy had begun years ago. To tell my story.

I rediscovered my passion, my joy for words, the excited flush rising to my face for the first time in decades.

The words I first wrote while sitting on my kitchen floor turned into my first book. About my life. Which eventually, amazingly, got published. And suddenly I was out, really out, not only to the world but also to Tate Academy. In a don't ask, don't tell world, I told without being asked, told without being tattled upon first. And, well, my rather flawed history didn't seem to mesh with the rather polished and perfected one of Tate's.

The truth of my situation finally hit me when an advance publicity article on me and my first book, *America's Boy*, appeared in our city newspaper. The book publicity came earlier than I had anticipated, and I panicked about how to announce the book, which I had kept a secret, just like my sexuality.

But it didn't matter how I tried to spin it this time, because my secret was already out to the world.

The first call I received summed up all the calls, summed up my earlier years with the M^2s, brought everything full circle. When I answered my phone, this M^2 said, "You have humiliated Tate Academy. The entire city. Obviously, you didn't attend this school. And you will be fired. *Faggot!*"

There it was, still ringing in my ear along with the slamming of the phone. That word. That hatred. Everything I had feared. Finally here for me to face in person.

And all from a mother.

Here they are. These are the people I work with every day, the "respectable, upstanding" upper class who are raising their children with "moral values." These are the people that boss me around, have me run their errands, and then rip me to shreds behind my back, whispering things—*whisper, whisper, whisper*—soft words and suspicious glances and analytical stares and shreds of conversations in damning tones that force me to hide in the dark, fearful that I'll be found out or fired or humiliated or something, I don't even know anymore.

"Faggot!"

That word keeps me silent. It has for years.

"Faggot!"

It is not the word, I know, but the hatred with which it is used, the "You are a filthy, God-hating, subhuman piece of trash." Period.

Still, my lowest point came when a little boy passed me in the hall and said, "Hello, Mr. Rouse!" And then he turned, his eyes glued to the floor, and said, "Oh, I just remembered. My parents said I'm not s'posed to talk to you 'cause you're bad."

A high point came when the faculty and staff organized my first unofficial book reading for *America's Boy,* and an overwhelming flood of great parents and alumni later showed to support me at my first official book signing. For once, I felt the support of a caring community and a pang of guilt for not sharing earlier the person I am. I carry that burden today.

But my highest point came when Mitsy called me at work. "Are you OK?" she asked me.

"I'm going to be," I said.

"So am I," this little girl, who was growing up so quickly, said. "I'm proud of you."

I had shared more with her in fewer words than I had with anyone in my life.

But it was at that moment I knew, I finally knew: I *had* made a difference. And this school, this faculty, the good parents were making a difference, too.

More than anything, however, I knew that it was simply time to go.

In the end, I gathered my office belongings and walked to my car, wishing I could carry an armload of troubled kids with me. On my final trek, arms loaded with boxes filled with framed certificates and my collection of Pez dispensers, I happened to pass the Mean Mommies of the four Barbies, who were now long gone from this old stomping ground. The Pink Ice Barbies still stood guard, however, forever protecting their turf in the carpool lane.

Whisper. Whisper. Whisper. Oh! My! God! was all I heard as I passed.

I scrunched into my car and started to drive away. But, as I did, I saw the M²s watching me, verbally dismantling me as they dramatically adjusted each other's pink-and-green Lilly Pulitzer skinny scarves and derby belts. Except for my outburst at Kitsy, I had never spoken out—against anyone—at Tate. Yet, I couldn't resist. I couldn't leave, this very last time, in silence.

I lowered the driver's window down and eased to a stop in the carpool lane—*my* carpool lane—in front of the Pink Ice Barbies. I began to speak. I already had my words planned. I was going to scream at them, "Ladies, I just thought you should know—pink is *so* last year. Actually so five years ago. And you really should choose a lipstick color that actually makes you look like you have lips. TTFN!"

But, ultimately, I couldn't. Because it finally hit me. If I did, I would have lost, and they would have won. If I did, I would not be leaving on my terms; I would be leaving on theirs. I couldn't because I finally realized the school was winning, the magnificent moms were crowding out the Mean Mommies. How did I know? No one, I realized, had chosen to replace Kitsy. Everyone I had worked with since had been incredible human beings. The M²s were the ones who were now isolated, clinging to the only thing they had left: this little patch of turf. And the Pink Ice Barbies were melting into a pool on their very own sidewalk.

So I kept my mouth shut and smiled, driving away from Tate Academy—yoga chanting one final time to center myself—watching the buildings' giant white columns grow smaller in my rearview window.

As I puttered my car back to my little brown house, I simply reminded myself that, after all, this is just school. The ultimate goal of Tate students, of all students, no matter their age, is to make it to Commencement: to graduate and then move onto bigger and better things, to realize that by leaving, you really get to start your own life, really get to begin changing the world, really get to affect history.

So that's exactly what I did.

Postscript

After I stopped working closely with Kitsy, I occasionally saw her around town, at the mall, or idling in her SUV at a stoplight, an aging LulaBelle riding shotgun wearing pink doggles, Kitsy gesturing wildly into her cell, Lucy and her canine version of Ethel out for a day of girlish fun. Not once, however, did Kitsy acknowledge my presence; it was as though she had never seen me, we had never met, never mind worked closely together.

However, the last time I saw Kitsy, one weekend morning, as Gary and I were sitting in the local coffeehouse, days before we were to move from this city and start our new lives in Michigan, she strolled in, a still-pink Laffy Taffy in heels. I slumped in my seat to avoid notice—old habits are hard to break—but Gary watched her closely, before kicking me under the table, his not-too-subtle sign that it was OK to look. Although I feared I would endure the same fate as Lot's wife if I did, I looked, and just at that moment, Kitsy turned toward me. She lowered her giant sunglasses and locked eyes with me, her frown morphing into just the slightest smile, like the Grinch. I nodded at her, but she was already turning.

Acknowledgments

When you work in isolation, alone in the middle of the woods, it takes a lot of people not only to keep you sane but also to transform your words into a book for the world to read. That is why thanks must be given to the following: first, to my editor, Julia Pastore, who believed in my work not just once, but twice. That will never be forgotten. To everyone at Harmony Books, for their hard work, expertise, and dedication. For my agent, Wendy Sherman, who continues to be my biggest fan, most loyal confidante, greatest cheerleader, and hardest worker. She's like Kathy Bates in *Misery* except sane, brilliant, well dressed, and gorgeous. Continued thanks to Michelle Brower. Thanks to all those who love me unconditionally in spite of my many faults, mistakes, and mood swings: Mom and Dad, you are my forever heroes; to all my new friends; to all my old friends; and to Gary and Marge, for everything, including hanging in there when times are tough, for keeping my feet warm, for going into the cave, and—most of all—for reminding me it's OK to be human and it's OK to grow old, especially when you're loved so deeply.

About the Author

WADE ROUSE is the author of the critically acclaimed memoir *America's Boy*, which was named a "Best Book of 2006" by Borders and the *St. Louis Post-Dispatch*. He is a contributor to a forthcoming humorous essay collection on working in retail, *The Customer Is Always Wrong*; and his essays and articles have appeared in numerous magazines. Wade earned his B.A. in communications from Drury University and his master's in journalism from Northwestern University. He lives on the coast of Michigan with his partner and their lovable mutt, Marge. In between blizzards and beach weather, he is working on his third memoir.

Visit him at www.waderouse.com or www.myspace.com/135803636.